Absolutely Adored

Stop Choosing Narcissistic Men and Finally Be a Well-Loved Woman

SIERRA FAITH

Contact:

DD

Dancing Deva Press

www.ConsciousCourtship.com
PuttingItIntoWords@gmail.com
P.O. Box 3067, Ashland, OR 97520

Interior design by Illumination Graphics

Softcover: ISBN 978-0-9985061-0-4
Ebook: ISBN 978-0-9985061-1-1

Dedication

For Donna Fletcher
with ever-lasting love

Table of Contents

Special thanks

I have had so much help and encouragement with this book. I wish to thank my close circle of friends who have been on my team for the eight years that it has taken to complete the project: Katherine Revoir, Michael Lighthawk, Kira Higgs, Shoshanna Alexander and Deborah Elliot. Also thanks to Leslie Keenan, Sharon Eisenhauer, Kristen Morrison, Mark Horowitz, Karen Wilson, Sky Canyon, Suzanne McQueen, Susan Garrett, Kiah Bosy, Deborah Perdue, and Naomi Saunders. A big thanks to Robin Stetcher for her generous spirit, and for extending her time, expertise, and feedback so graciously. I thank Brenda Shipley for approaching me with the idea and insisting that I write the book. I bow to Laurie Boucher for her beautiful cover image, and invite you to visit her photographs online, laurielynboucher.com. Big thanks to Alisa Armstrong who was a client turned editor, and to her unique understanding of my work, coupled with her professional expertise. Much gratitude to all of the people who offered their financial and moral support toward the publication of this book, especially Margy Stewart. And I would especially like to express appreciation to all of my clients who have allowed me to accompany them on their romantic journeys. You are my greatest teachers.

Appreciation

I wish to acknowledge four other coaches from whom I have learned so much and borrowed so freely. Their ideas have become woven into mine. I will make reference to them, and other experts in the field, throughout the book. But I wish to shine a spotlight on these coaches now, since my work would not exist in its best version without their brilliance.

John Gray
Katherine Woodward Thomas
Alison Armstrong
Dr. Patricia Allen

Thank you.

Introduction

*A*s you read this book we will be taking a journey together. It is a journey that will lead you away from patterns that have not served you, patterns that have inevitably resulted in frustrating and unfulfilling romantic relationships. The destination of this journey is a deep level of feminine homecoming that will equip you with the understanding, wisdom, and hands-on experience necessary to find the love you want.

If you're anything like me, you may want to skip to the how-to information in Part Two. However, Part One includes important principles and critical understanding that will support you in creating an entirely new set point as you begin to date again. I encourage you to read the material in the order it is presented so that you're fully prepared to do things differently, and thus get the new and effective results that you're looking for.

In the first part of the book we will take a look at the obstacles that have kept you from the kind of love that you want and deserve, and examine how the past may have colored your experience. We will also clearly define the kind of men you *don't* want, and the kind of men who are *good* for you.

Many women actually believe that if they could just find the right guy everything would be great. They want to meet "Him," skip the whole "dating thing," and plunge into an exclusive relationship. That game plan often sows the seeds for disappointment down the line, because women, too often, are acting out of old patterns that keep inviting in the wrong guys. So, as we begin, we will look at some new models of healthy romantic interaction, and elevate your skills for attracting men that are the right fit for the new, healthy you.

The second section of *Absolutely Adored* will get these fresh awarenesses on their feet through a very specific process of online dating. That process will allow you to vet men up front so that you can weed out the narcissistic guys and choose men who will be good to you. We'll walk through creating profiles, initial emails, phone calls, and first and second dates. This section will require some time, patience, and a little faith as you explore unfamiliar territory. However, as you learn these new principles, and practice a new set of skills and techniques, you'll find that you begin to interact with a new kind of man.

The third part of the book adds depth and breadth to your understanding and appreciation of men. These chapters will allow you to finesse your skills as a feminine woman who enjoys and encourages the healthy masculine.

The last part of *Absolutely Adored* is more about you and your path to feminine fulfillment.

Scattered throughout this book are opportunities to attain new levels of self-reflection and self-assessment. You will be challenged to rethink habitual patterns of thought and behavior, and your self-esteem may encounter some up-leveling. But the process is gentle and clear, and you will be in charge of the intensity and velocity of the ride. It is impossible to find and anchor yourself in this new paradigm without staying in close touch with your feelings. As you proceed, you will develop an increasingly sensitive internal barometer that will guide and inform you.

It is my expectation that you will find yourself at an entirely new level of confidence and romantic fulfillment by the time you finish reading and applying the tools and principles contained in *Absolutely Adored*.

Enjoy the ride.

Preface

Smart women who were raised by self-centered parents often have problems in romantic relationships. Either they don't know how to choose men who will treat them well, or they get involved in relationships that start out with a bang but eventually deconstruct as their men become more and more complacent. Those women are missing some key pieces of knowledge, understanding, and behavior necessary to creating a healthy, happy, sustainable romantic dynamic. If I am describing you, read on because this book offers the missing pieces of the puzzle.

There are many experts who write about dating and creating effective romantic relationships. All of these tools and teachers are invaluable resources for women who want to experience romantic gratification. And they are incredibly effective *if those women come from a healthy base of self-esteem and self-nurturing, and a clear, organic reference point of deep self-worth.*

However, for women who were taught from an early age to care for their caretakers' needs first, and were groomed to believe that being an adept "giver" was how they would thrive and survive, that healthy base of feminine self-esteem is often damaged. Such girls can grow into women who believe that their true worth is measured by their ability to give. When these women experience the good fortune to encounter a man who asks that they deeply *receive* without the need for reciprocity – something foreign to their care-giving nature – they often crash. When their own relaxation and receptivity are seminal aspects of what's required in a healthy romantic dynamic, here comes the vertigo: fear, misunderstanding, compulsive self-sufficiency, cynicism, and control can emerge, followed by disillusionment and resignation. All of this results in the *"I knew this thing was a fairy tale"* mindset.

It's a terrible feeling to see others succeeding where we have failed, especially if we pride ourselves on being women who can figure anything and everything out.

What is the barrier that keeps us from our own success in a romantic relationship? What can we do to "succeed" in this new and foreign arena?

This book helps women define and break through that barrier. It is a blueprint for the behavioral and neurological shift necessary for women who want to be able to attract, and interact with, generous, cherishing men. As such, it is not a "how to do" book but a "how to be" book – how to be receptive and ready to receive those generous, cherishing men.

Furthermore, this book uses online dating as a classroom for learning and experiencing a new paradigm, with definite tools and skill sets.

"Dang! Not online dating! Been there, done that. It's painful and disappointing, and a time-consuming drag. It's for losers! Anything but that!"

Online dating is a neutral, and often extremely effective medium for meeting many different kinds of men. *Absolutely Adored* uses this medium as a gateway for education, examination, and exercising the new skills necessary to create and sustain successful romantic relationships. I think you'll find, as so many of my clients have, that a new and rewarding experience awaits you as you take this journey with an open mind and an open heart.

Prelude – My Story

*I*n 1999 I decided to try online dating. I had been single for six years, during which time I'd been healing some unhealthy romantic patterns. I'd done a lot of work on myself, and felt ready to meet a man. Like a lot of women, I really didn't know how to find the right guy, and I went about it with the thought that *finding the right guy was the goal*. I was raised by narcissistic and abusive parents who had a very dysfunctional marriage, and they had nothing to offer in the way of healthy romantic modeling. As a result of that upbringing I spent the better part of three decades in 12-Step meetings, therapists' offices, and sessions with healers of many different kinds trying to become a functional, balanced woman. My work was thorough, and eventually I felt like I had succeeded in transforming my poison into medicine. I was beautiful and smart. What's not to love?

I filled out a profile on Match.com, shooting from the hip, with an attractive black and white headshot, and ran it up the flagpole.

My results were mixed. I was less than excited about who saluted, and I often felt insecure or disappointed when I viewed the men who had contacted me.

Then a friend introduced me to John Gray's book, *Mars and Venus on a Date*. I was very reticent about reading it. In some circles they would call my attitude "contempt before investigation." After all, I already *knew* a lot. I knew how to communicate clearly and responsibly.

I knew how to be emotionally present and fluent. I knew how to be honest and create rewarding friendships. I knew about the power of consciousness, and how deeply our beliefs influence the contours of our life. I knew myself. I didn't want to play games, and I thought that's what John Gray would be talking about: how to manipulate men. But my friend was enthusiastic, and seemed to be enjoying what she was learning, so I rolled with it.

Wow. Was I ever wrong.

This information wasn't about learning to manipulate men. This was about learning to *understand* men, and the dating process, and I quickly began to discover what I *didn't* know: I didn't know that there *was* a dating process, I didn't know that there were stages of dating, I didn't know that there were men out there whose sole aim was to cherish me, I didn't know what it meant to be cherished, and I certainly didn't know how to recognize those guys. And, as Alison Armstrong puts it, I didn't know that men weren't "big, hairy, defective women."

I didn't know jack.

My friend wanted to apply what we were reading to our online dating experience. We teamed up and began discussing the principles and debriefing with each other as we met and interacted with men. We also added to our study Dr. Patricia Allen's book, *Getting to I Do*. After reading that book I went back and reassessed my profile in light of this new body of knowledge. I was horrified to see how clueless my initial writing had been.

Perhaps the most stunning revelation that I experienced from my studies was recognizing the difference between generous, cherishing men and more narcissistic men. I saw that I was habitually attracted to the second category, and had created a profile designed to attract them.

Whoa.

I changed that immediately, and soon I began to be able to distinguish between these two types of guys by the way they approached me, and by the content of their pictures and profiles.

I also began to understand early dating, with its emphasis on fun, optimism, and spaciousness. I, for sure, had never done this. I formerly chose men based on chemistry, dove deep, fast, bonded quickly, and ended up clueless, confused, unhappy, and highly adrenalized, quickly: quickly engaged and quickly wrecked by that engagement. Frankly, it had never occurred to me to vet the men who approached me by moving slowly, keeping my head, focusing on fun, having short dates with a lot of space in between, and then having time to see how I felt and whether or not I wanted to see them again. I had never really *dated*. And I certainly had never dated several men at the same time, which I learned was often a part of a healthy dating strategy for women like me.

I was learning, learning, learning, and it was glorious because I'm a very loving, sensual, relational woman, and I was *finally* getting a blueprint for healthy romance.

Gradually I started becoming attracted to a new kind of man – cherishing men – and found that spending time with them was fun and raised my self-esteem. I felt much more relaxed, confident, and beautiful with them. I started really loving these guys. As time went on, I read more, attended some workshops given by great coaches, and I continued to practice. I liked dating. It was fun, and such a relief after decades of hot chemistry, deep fast dives, enmeshment, and unhappiness. I could breathe. I was more in control of my instincts, and I was navigating them in the light of more expansive education and new experiences.

There was one man in particular who really taught me what a joy it is to date a generous, cherishing man. My heart opened to him. I was very aware of the stages of dating, and consciously navigated them. He was very masculine, fun, funny, and he deeply adored and explored me in a manner I had not experienced before, which was glorious. However, after five months it was clear that there were some non-negotiable differences between us in the area of spiritual compatibility and sexual chemistry. So I broke things off with him, and then had the rewarding experience of grieving without any blame or shame – just letting my heart feel and heal.

At that point I stopped dating for a while, shut down my online profiles, moved to Hawaii, and finished writing a novel. During that time a friend approached me and asked me to teach her what I had learned during my recent dating years. I agreed. She referred more women to me and I began my work as a dating and relationship coach. Since then I have coached many clients, both women and men. I have helped them step into healthy relationships, sometimes stepping all the way into marriage. My tandem work as a creative mentor, spiritual coach, and an intuitive plays into my relationship coaching, and I am constantly expanding my research and experience. And I, myself, have continued dating on and off.

Up to now, my writing and my clients have been my focus, and I have not yet felt ready to create a significant romantic relationship in my own life. So, although I haven't met my guy yet, lots of my clients have, following the guidance in this book. And I have no doubt that when I'm ready, my time will come.

PART 1:

Preparing for the Process

"I consider myself to be a thoughtful and aware person, yet so much about dating and relationship was not intuitive for me. As a result of my work with Sierra, I came to see some of my assumptions and behaviors with men as confused and self-defeating. With her help I was able to make adjustments that resulted in a wonderful outcome. A year and a half ago, I met a man online with whom I'm having the happiest, healthiest relationship of my life."

Rachel

As we begin, let's take a look at you – who you are and how you have attempted to find a satisfying love life in the past. Let's also look at what you know, and what you probably *don't* know, about men and how to create fulfilling romance.

This will be a time to self-assess, challenge some long-held beliefs, and then put some new pieces in place as preparation for doing things differently.

Note: In the following chapters I will be teaching about narcissism in parents and in potential suitors. I will be referring to unhealthy, destructive narcissism.

1

A Word About Being Groomed
by Narcissistic Parents

Healthy children are raised, in general, by healthy parents, parents who understand that they are there to attend to the needs of their children, and not vice versa. Healthy children have to be cared for in a manner that allows them to form healthy attachments with themselves, their parents, the outside world, and possibly the God of their understanding. Based on my research and understanding I define the elements of healthy attachments as consistency, congruence, contingency, and companioning.

(When I use the word "you" in the following definitions, it's from the perspective of a child. When children have strong healthy attachments, they will translate those attachments to their relationships with themselves, others, their concept of a Supreme Being, and to life itself.)

1. Consistency: You are regularly there for me. I am the child, and you are the adult, and you have your eye on my well-being. You anticipate my needs, and you respond promptly to my desire for your presence. You keep your agreements and promises with me.
Result: **I know that you will provide for me. I come to expect well-being and loving provision as the norm. I feel esteemed and happy.**

2. Congruence: I can count on you to be the same person each time I encounter you: a good, loving, cheerful, and cherishing person; no big mood swings, personality changes, or sudden shifts in our reality base mid-stream.
Result: **I feel relaxed, confident, and comfortable relating to you.**

3. Contingency: You've got my back. You protect me, support me in many ways, and prevent others from harming me.
Result: **I feel safe and secure in your care, and I know that you will help me, and that things will work out well.**

4. Companioning: You meet me where I am at, at any given time. Whether I am sad, or excited, or scared, or inspired, you find your way to my reality, and accompany me in my experience with your love, attention, and the best you've got to give. We talk easily with respect and reciprocity.
Result: **I feel clear about my own feelings and perceptions. I trust and value my instincts and experience. I share them and listen to yours.**

Most of my clients were not raised by such parents. If that happens to be the case for you, you may have been emotionally groomed to take care of your parents needs before your own. There is much to say about this, and, because I am not a trained therapist, I will only address how this kind of childhood grooming shows up in my work.

Frequently women who were raised in this manner experience upside-down results when it comes to attachment while dating.

Instead of *Consistency* the childhood attachment is:
1. *Inconsistent:* Maybe you'll show up, maybe you won't. Maybe you'll take me to the park, or make me dinner, or change my diaper like you said you would and should, maybe you won't. You randomly neglect me or disappear.
Adult Result: Instead of **I know you will provide for me. I come to expect well-being and loving provision as the norm. I feel esteemed and happy...**
"If you provide for me it's because you expect something in return. I don't trust you to care for me, and I must depend upon myself. I feel like I have to prove my worth, and I am tired and stressed."

Instead of *Congruence* the childhood attachment is:
2. *Incongruent:* I never know who you'll be when I next encounter you: mood swings, personality changes, emotional swings, unpredictable, scary. Maybe you'll like me, maybe you won't.
Adult Result: Instead of **I feel relaxed, confident, and comfortable relating to you...**
"I feel tense, insecure, hyper-vigilant, and uncomfortable relating to you."

Instead of *Contingency* the childhood attachment is:
3. *I'm on my own:* I'm in trouble, or scared, or lost, or confused, and you're either nowhere to be found or you don't care. You might even belittle me, or make fun of my feelings or needs.
Adult Result: Instead of **I feel safe and secure in your care, and I expect that you will help me and that things will work out well...**
"I have to watch my back. If you provide for or protect me, I am disbelieving and on the lookout for the price I'm going to pay. Or, I am so grateful that you're nice to me that I want to give back in kind, ASAP."

Instead of Companioning the childhood attachment is:
4. *I'm alone in my experience:* I'm having many feelings and interactions and thoughts throughout my day, and you either don't ask me about myself and my experiences, or you invalidate, demean, shame, or ignore my inner life, or both. You talk at me, not with me.
Adult Result: Instead of **I feel clear about my own feelings and perceptions. I trust and value my instincts and experience...**
"I am often out of touch with my own feelings because I'm so involved with reading you, and your needs and feelings. I don't trust my perceptions. Or, if I do trust my instincts, it's because they are jaded and suspicious, and are there to protect me from your inevitable abandonment. I keep my thoughts to myself."
Not so good.

Many women have come to believe that all men are inherently narcissistic, and that they judge women based on how well they think those women will fulfill their needs. These women believe that all men are self-centered, selfish, and only want two things: sex and power. Many women project the self-centeredness of their primary caretakers onto men, and end up hurt, exhausted, and very, very angry.

Learning that, in fact, there are many men who are generous and cherishing, men who are fulfilled by studying and increasing the happiness of women, comes as a shock. Certainly women can find narcissistic men out there. But there are just as many, if not more, generous, cherishing men. Knowing how to recognize them, and allowing them to recognize you, is another matter. That, in many ways, is the heart of my work.

2

What's in it for Me? Why Online Dating?

Fair question, especially since you may have tested the waters before and been less than delighted with the results. If you are like most of my clients, you are a high-performance woman who habitually "over-gives" (a trait and mindset that I will address in depth later.) Most probably, you have centered your criteria for potential dates around compatibility *(we have the same interests and values)* and chemistry *(I like the way he looks)*. AND, when you find yourself in the presence of a man with whom you share compatibility and feel chemistry, your over-giving kicks in, which perpetuates disappointment with, and misinterpretation of, men.

I find that online dating is a very useful medium for learning new dating skills and perspectives because you can move slowly, and actually freeze-frame the process in the beginning stages. That kind of control means that you have the opportunity to learn and integrate new ways of seeing and sorting through potential suitors, and then practice new ways of interacting with them, and yourself, with a sense of spaciousness. Plus, there is the bonus of volume of traffic, which means that you are less likely to make any one man too precious or important. And, lastly, the anonymity factor supports risk and exper- imentation, and allows you to play with the manner in which you present yourself, through pictures and text, in service to your learning curve. So you get to control the speed and velocity of the process, interact with lots of men, and update and raise your skill level and presentation in an atmosphere of trial and error.

If you were just looking for the right guy, maybe online dating would serve you and maybe it wouldn't. (Current Pew studies show that up to one third of the couples married in the last ten years met online, and that marriages that started online report a higher level of marital satisfaction than those that did not. *I'm just sayin'*.) But in this dance, it's about you learning how to become a woman who is capable of recognizing and receiving the right guy, and online dating is conducive to successfully achieving that goal. And, along the way, the right guy may show up, and if he does, you're much more prepared to launch. And even if he doesn't, this process will create a woman who is much happier in her own skin, with or without a man. I always find with my clients that the happier they are within themselves, the more likely a man is apt to appear at just the right moment. And oddly, and wonderfully, not before.

So let's get to it!

3

Masculine and Feminine Energy

There is a uniquely feminine energy and a uniquely masculine energy that play themselves out in the romantic arena.

Feminine energy is self-loving, joyously receptive, and thrives on receiving. This energy becomes depleted when it has to give too much, and becomes energized, and actually falls in love, when it is cherished, protected, and provided for.

Masculine energy has a need to give, it likes to work for what it earns, and it thrives on creating discernible happiness for feminine energy. This energy becomes vibrant and amplified when it has to work for its goals, which plays itself out as "chasing space" during courtship. (More about this idea will be elaborated upon in upcoming chapters.) Masculine energy also needs to experience safety, warmth, joy, optimism, and receptivity in the feminine energy with which it interacts. Masculine energy falls in love when it successfully gives in a manner that creates sustained happiness for its partner.

In the romantic dance there needs to be a masculine energy and a feminine energy, as described above. A woman can be the masculine energy, and a man can easily be the feminine energy. But for our purposes, we will be looking to develop the healthy feminine in you, and we will be looking to attract men who embody healthy masculine energy. Henceforth, I will refer to these kind of men as *"masculine men," or "MMs."*

(The principles of this work can translate to same sex couples. Because that is not my strongest area of expertise, this book is geared toward heterosexual women.)

Masculine Men (MMs)

I want to pause here and briefly describe these men, because this is where we're going. These are the guys who will treat you like a queen.

These men will protect, provide for, and cherish you. They are optimistic, happy, and self-fulfilled. They have a great deal of dignity, and they are generous by nature. And there are lots of them out there, but you probably have not recognized them because of your imbedded perspectives – perspectives we will examine and dissect in detail as we move farther into this journey. The whole thrust of this book is to allow you to begin to recognize, attract, and interact with these guys as potential suitors.

Because you are unaccustomed to seeing and considering them as romantic partners, you can expect to be in a process of personal change that may feel foreign or uncomfortable at times. It may be a small series of tremors, and it may be a substantial seismic shift.

Oh well.

You have probably had to go through many such processes in your life as you grow and evolve in the direction of your dreams.

There will be lots of information about these men in upcoming chapters. But I just wanted to give you a clear preview of the bar we are setting.

5

Excuses

I'm too old.
It's too late.
All the good men are already taken.

Let's just handle these now, okay?

1. I'm too old.

I don't think so. If you're over 90 (really) it gets a little trickier, but even then it's not impossible. Shy of that, this is a fantastic time to meet and even marry – at any age. I currently have a number of clients who are enjoying the best romantic relationships of their lives, many of them in their 60s and 70s. All of them have met their guys in the last two years. They are involved with quality, masculine men, and it's really, really good: the sex is good, the communication is good, the courtship is fantastic. These are happy gals. You can be one, too.

2. It's too late.

I don't think so. You can do this, even if you've never had a great relationship before, or if you think that your lifestyle is intractable, or you've tried and failed before. You can learn how to create a wonderful relationship with a wonderful man. It's only too late if you say so. Otherwise life will support you if you let it, and if you use the available resources.

3. All the good ones are already taken.

So not true. Just because you haven't met them doesn't mean that they're not out there. You're going to learn how to see them, understand them, attract them, and interact with them. If you're more mature, you have the extra-added bonus of often meeting great guys who were married for many years and then lost their wives. These are men who love being in relationship and are good at it. Overall, online dating has revolutionized our access to each other. There are millions of men online, on many different dating sites, who want a great relationship with a wonderful woman just like you. Give it a shot. In this case it will be fun to be wrong.

6

Women are Smarting

I was doing a spell check on my writing this morning and the computer asked me if I wanted to change the title of one of my chapters from "Women are Smart" to "Women are Smarting." At first I laughed. Then I recognized the poignant truth of that correction. I know what it feels like to be a smart woman who watches other women love, and be loved, by a man in a manner that seems so out of reach. It's frustrating to be so capable in so many ways, and so apparently clueless or unsuccessful when it comes to love. A sad fact is that many smart women conclude that, because they've experienced their own capability in so many other areas of their life, and they can't get what they want romantically by applying that capability, then what they want must be a myth.

That smarts.

7

Women are Smart

Most women are resourceful, ingenious, and creative. We've often needed to figure out how to navigate in a predominantly masculine energy model in many aspects of our lives. We've had to learn how to care for ourselves, and create money, and homes, and families, and support systems, not to mention balance, self-care, and integrity. Men often teach other men the attitudes, strategies, and behaviors that will render them successful in a man's world, but not many women get that kind of education handed to them. Of course, if we were living in a society that based its models on intuition and the cycles of nature, and was nurturing, sustainable, and communal, and was also governed by win-win principles, most women would instinctively flourish. For most of us that has not been the case.

I'm not bemoaning the values of western culture, but merely making a point that, in our paradigm, as women, we've had to develop and emphasize a certain set of perspectives and skills in order to survive and become autonomous, balanced, and successful.

And that's good! We can do that. We parlay our feminine values of honesty and integrity, and anticipating and accommodating each other's needs, and planning, and reciprocity, and generosity, and initiative, and clear, forthright communication and hard work into thriving lives. We create careers and strong social networks. We become self-generating, self-correcting, and independent. We've got it covered. And the more adept we are at managing our lives, the more fortified and confident we become in our own knowledge and wisdom about how things work...

'Cause they're workin'...

Mostly...

Where this system can break down is in the metaphorical bedroom. Most men don't want to be challenged by, competed with, or managed by their romantic partners. And, truth be told, most women lose respect for men who do.

Oops…

Dr. Patricia Allen calls what needs to happen being "masculine in the boardroom and feminine in the bedroom." I call it challenging. To learn how to shift into a feminine receptive mode with romantic partners in a way that does not feel like some gigantic sacrifice of power and authenticity, and *does* feel natural, organic, and delicious is a rewarding new learning curve, with two prominent challenges leading the parade. So I will summarize those challenges as elegantly and expediently as possible, and, hopefully, you will identify.

1. Challenge #1: Being Too Smart

The biggest and most immediate challenge that most of my clients face when it comes to learning how to more effectively attract and interact with men is that *they think they already know.*

Having created and orchestrated a personal world that works in many ways, smart, ingenious, capable women assume that if they just do what they've been doing in their other successful relationships with friends, work associates, and families, their romantic lives should also flourish. And if their romantic lives *aren't* flourishing, these women assume that either they need to do *more* of what they've been doing elsewhere, or they just haven't found the right guy. It's the "*I just want to be exactly who I am and find a guy who loves me that way*" school of dating. And, in most cases, the more capable the woman, the more they are married to their methodology.

So what have we been doing that's working out there in the world? Well, elsewhere in our successful relationships…

- We have been initiating with time, plans, ideas, personnel, and solutions.

- We're often "up" people. We freely give compliments, and we're effusive. In fact, we often place a high premium on our self-image as people who reach out and connect, allowing others to do so as well.

- We are very competent, and we pride ourselves on feeling powerful, and equal to, our male counterparts, easily able to hold our own when we're with them. We can be the confident leader in a team that includes men.

- We thrive on respect.

- We've worked hard to define ourselves: resolving childhood issues and addictions, developing our interpersonal skills, and clarifying our passions and strengths. We put a great emphasis on transparency. We are forthcoming; what you see is what you get.

- We value reciprocity and fairness. We are quick to keep a tally on what's been given to us, and make sure that we respond in kind and keep the ledger even.

- We've learned to be polite and gracious. We want to spare others from expending any unnecessary effort on our behalf.

Of their own accord all of these qualities, attitudes, and behaviors are useful, constructive and positive. What many women don't understand is that they are all primarily *masculine energy* qualities, attitudes, and behaviors when exercised in the romantic paradigm. And because we have invested so much of ourselves into mastering this way of being in the world, we are often deeply identified with these roles. We don't know that there are essential pieces of our femininity which have been lost in the mix – pieces like receptivity, diffused focus, and becoming pleasure-centered. Sometimes we actually judge and condemn those lost aspects of ourselves, when, in fact, they are the keys to the queendom. So when I come along and begin to suggest that there is an entire platform of self-image and interaction that infers that they *don't know,* women can feel rebellious, overwhelmed, suspicious, or grandiose.

The issue is that many women have become so accustomed to presenting, creating, and managing with their more masculine energies that they believe *this is who they are,* and both the idea and the experience of beginning to shift into more feminine energy feels phony, difficult, dicey, and often scary. (Remember that, romantically speaking, feminine energy is initially characterized by magnetism, relaxing, loving and enjoying ourselves, and letting men try and win us.) We have learned to work for the results, and often the love, in our lives. We actually believe that what makes us loveable is our constellation of masculine traits. We may not think that we can attract some fabulous man just because of "little ol' me," and we are missing the self-esteem to know that we are worthy of deep cherishing because of who we are rather than what we bring to the table. So it seems perfectly natural that if we want to find the right guy, we'll just roll up our sleeves, focus our energy and intention, and get our game on.

Unfortunately, that kind of approach is often a full-throttle green light for a narcissistic man who will be looking for women who can please *him,* rather than vice versa.

This is an illustration of what I mean – think back on your own childhood. If you happen to have been raised by one or more parents who were somewhat narcissistic – e.g., asked you to take care of their feelings before your own, made you the "little man or little woman" of the house, taught you to walk on eggshells, or in some way "groomed" you to make sure that their needs were taken care of before yours were addressed – your tendency to over-give may be deeply embedded.

And therefore, interacting with more narcissistic men may feel comfortable, and even familial. I find that women who fall into this category of upbringing can find the principles of my work very challenging, initially. However, once they become willing to try them, these same women are often the clients who are most transformed. The challenging principles become a doorway to pleasure, freedom, and feminine homecoming.

So the upside of having learned how to maximize masculine energy is a feeling of control, independence, and success. The downside is a form of feminine exhaustion and depletion. There are so many deep needs that don't get met, and, in many cases, are never even named or acknowledged, when women give too much and don't exercise their profound capacity for receiving and being deeply, creatively loved and cherished. Such women might become harsh, brittle, cynical, hyper-controlling, and perfectionist. They also can swing into workaholism or compulsive behaviors in the area of care-taking and consumption (co-dependence, shopping, overeating, etc.)

Here's what a lifetime of this can breed – there's something we need that we're so accustomed to *not* getting that we often *don't even know that it exists.*

Meanwhile, there is a whole team of men who are eager to give it to us, and *we don't even see them.* We don't recognize their masculinity because we have formed prejudices against them, or we are so used to going into battle with them that we never take the armor off long enough to find out who we are and who they are. Consequently, we often have come to objectify men, and think of them as expendable boy toys. We might view romantic relationships as a take-away rather than an add-on. We go into our love lives misinformed, misdirected, and cocky or defeated. And somehow we're surprised when we don't feel good.

Oy vey.

If we don't know who we are, and what we need, as women, then we act like men, (leading, pursuing, over-giving, putting the guys at ease, taking care of their feelings, becoming single-focused) which doesn't work. Meanwhile, we expect men to think and act like women (be feeling-focused, easily access their heart, be able to multi-task, be able to track our experience and know what we want without having to tell them, etc.). This strategy leaves everyone unfulfilled, and adds to the cynical myth that the kind of love we desire is some Cinderella-complex fairy tale that doesn't happen in the real world.

The good news is: you're wrong.

The challenging news is: you're wrong.

There is a huge population of men out there who want nothing more than to succeed at making you happy, and your job is to let them.

What all of this sifts down to is that not only are you going to learn to recognize and attract generous, cherishing men, but you're going to recognize and begin to reveal your own feminine nature as you do it.

So this work isn't just about cracking the code in *them*. You're going to have *your* code cracked, and you're probably going to change.

The old game was: find a man who will act the way I want him to, i.e., like a great woman friend would act.

New rules: you get to start becoming and acting like the deeply feminine woman that you actually are, and let the guys be guys.

It's possible you're thinking that what I'm proposing is some disempowered, retro model of sexual politics that spells the loss of your integrity, authenticity, and power, all so some self-centered egomaniac will finally bring you flowers and pay for dinner.

Think again…

2. Challenge #2: Exposing the Soft Underbelly

The second challenge of this work is that a woman can feel unexpectedly vulnerable as she disarms herself and becomes receptive. After girding our loins in order to stay empowered in the presence of powerful men, and after learning to organize our energy and thinking to stabilize that position, the release of control can bring up deep feelings, emotional shifts, fear, and sometimes even unresolved childhood issues. It may also be surprising and/or humiliating to find out that your self-esteem around dating isn't what you thought it was. This vulnerability results in women having the idea that they don't want, or like, to date. They just want to meet the right guy and go straight into an exclusive relationship. When women date a number of men, and emotionally invest slowly, they're forced up against lots of self-worth issues that never peek out if they just skip the whole thing and get into relationship quickly. That is one of the primary reasons that I encourage women to do this thing right, consciously and deliberately moving through the stages of dating, allowing themselves the gifts of discovery and homecoming that can profoundly stabilize their self-esteem for the long run. So know that this is not just another cognitive manual to be read and implemented. Gather a gentle net of support around you, and know that you may hit some vertigo as you begin to sit back and let men lead.

- *Vulnerability is good when you're with a man who is healthy and who honors you.*
- *Vulnerability is eventually fun when it's a **voluntary vulnerability** because you've wisely chosen a man who knows how to lead and who grooves on your happiness.*
- *Vulnerability is ecstatic when it's safe and progressive. It's all about opening up to receive more cherishing than you ever knew was possible.*

Even though you may have doubts, let's give it a shot and see what happens in *your* love life, *your* own vitality, and *your* sense of self.

Is this going to be easy?

Maybe not so much.

But doable? Yes. And since women can do anything, let's get to it!

8

A Few Heads Ups

Let's talk about what to expect as you begin this journey.

1. Expect to be engaging in a path that requires time, energy, focus, and willingness.

2. Expect to encounter the need to get your words and your pictures right before you launch an online profile. I can't emphasize strongly enough the payoff for presenting yourself clearly as a feminine woman according to the guidelines I'm going to lay out. It can take a few weeks, and some trial and error. The days of, *"Maybe they're not quite right, but these photos are good enough,"* and, *"Well, this text is close enough. I'm sick of this process, and if they can't tell who I am when I lay it all out there, then screw it,"* are over. Do it right. Men are highly visual, and they want to pursue a woman who is clearly letting them know, in language and images they understand, that she is a woman who is available for cherishing. And they're often "first impressions, last impressions" creatures. Let's say you throw up a profile with pictures your friends like, and text that expects men to think like women, and then you discover down the road that maybe there was something to what I'm saying. By the time you re-format your profile, a whole bunch of guys who looked at your old profile will probably never re-visit the new one, and you may have been passed over by some winners who won't be back for a second look.

3. Expect that this will take time. It's best to release speedy timelines about finding the right guy. Negotiate impatience. Current studies show that, for most women who met their husbands online, it took at least six months of dating before they found each other, and sometimes up to a year. If you were starting a new business, you'd give it at least a year to begin showing a profit, right? And surely finding your guy, if you believe he exists (and he does) is as important as a new business in the bigger scheme of things. So develop realistic expectations about the process. Generally, most women are in a significant learning curve for the first three or four months of doing this work. And because the universe responds to intention, I believe that we get what we need for as long as we need it when our intentions are clear. So know that you'll probably interact with the right men in order to learn what you need to learn as you go along. When you're ready, the "A" list players will show up.

4. Expect to pace yourself. If you can, I suggest you enlist a dating buddy who will either do this process along with you, or will at least do weekly check-ins with you. Clearly outline your goals and your weekly actions with this person so that you have both a partner for accountability and a trusting friend who can be there for support, encouragement, and debriefing.

Note: Since you may be engaging in a very different way of online dating than your friends might advocate, make sure you don't choose a buddy who's going to constantly challenge your decision to do this, or question or criticize my guidance. Choose someone who will share this walk out on the skinny branches of the unknown, and who will be open to supporting your adventure as it unfolds.

9

A Word about Advice

I'm all for taking the love life advice of your good friends as long as they have what you want. If you admire the happy, stabile, delightful romantic relationship that they're engaged in, with a partner who adores them, treats them like a queen, and has his own life and affairs together, then by all means listen to them. But if you have wonderful friends who are *not* experiencing deep joy and being treasured, or who are not experts in this field, I suggest that you do not go to that well to drink. Please consider the source. No criticism intended. They just may not know how to invest in a full, healthy romantic partnership.

10

Success Watermarks

This is a big journey into unfamiliar territory. It's important to put in place some rest stops where you pause, assess, and acknowledge your progress. Long-term success (for example meeting, dating, and perhaps marrying your "it" guy) will be comprised of many incremental successes along the way. Celebrating each of those smaller successes will build stamina and self-esteem. These "success watermarks" are also good times to decide whether or not you want to continue on this journey. I find that surveying the path I'm walking, from a vantage point of the successes to date, keeps me levelheaded and self-compassionate.

Throughout this book I will note some success watermarks. At each of them I invite you to take a timeout and reflect on your progress and your feelings. Commit to the dance and then check in with some milestones.

First let's turn our attention to the definition of a healthy relationship, and what that looks like.

11

The Five Cs: Chemistry, Compatibility, Communication, Courtship, and Consciousness

I believe that all of these elements need to be present for a complete and fulfilling romantic union to occur.

Chemistry: The x factor that causes us to be sexually, intellectually, emotionally, and spiritually attracted to a potential mate. It may be challenging to develop if it's not immediately present. However, if a small flame of chemistry exists, often that flame can be fanned into a much bigger fire through the process of satisfying and progressive dating and courtship. Often women associate the idea of chemistry with physical attraction, but it is much more than that. And you may find that physical attraction is deeply impacted by courtship and how well a man treats you.

Compatibility: Both a short and long-term congruence of interests, lifestyle, ethics, ideas, goals, cosmology, and personal style that paves the way for great companionship and partnership.

Communication: How we interact through verbal and non-verbal cues and skills in a manner that promotes clear, healthy, comprehensive connection with, and understanding of, one another.

Courtship: The romantic dance that allows both participants to access and expand their respective masculine and feminine natures in relationship to one another. This dance builds excitement, energy, joy, and attraction, and paves the way for a lifetime of bonding and devotion, both emotional and erotic. Big Fun.

Consciousness: This element is pretty much home base for all relationships. It is, in essence, how we organize, focus, and steward our beliefs, thoughts, perceptions, and emotions. It is an offshoot of compatibility and communication, but is more than that. It is the foundation that creates and frames our understanding and experience of ourselves, others, and life itself.

All of these elements need not be present in order to have a fulfilling *dating* experience. In fact, when women are in the process of becoming re-educated about men and courtship, it is often preferable *not* to have all of these elements present. You're going to learn how to keep your head, relax, feel, observe, vet, and consciously practice new ways of thinking, behaving, perceiving, and assessing. If you're with a man with whom there is substantial chemistry and compatibility going on, often the old attitudes and behaviors, e.g., trying to please him, taking care of his feelings, and losing touch with your own sense of pleasure and timing, kick in pretty quickly because you like him and want him to like you. So, in the beginning we will put our focus on the courtship and communication aspects of this dance (how he treats you and communicates with you, and how you feel as a result) with consciousness weaving in when possible. Later, when you're more secure in your feminine skills, you'll have a little more neurological ballast to keep you grounded as more chemistry and compatibility play a bigger part in your interactions.

However, I wanted to present you with a clear description of the desired destination, romantically speaking, so that you could have a vision of what's to come.

12

The Five Stages of Dating

I will freely borrow from John Gray's book, *Mars and Venus on a Date*. Please read that book for a much more comprehensive model of the dating stages. This book is primarily concerned with stage one dating because it is the stage that many women want to skip, and this stage actually forms the platform on which a long-term healthy romance sits. Without it, the rest of the process is handicapped. However, I think it's worthwhile to have an overview of how the rest of this rolls in the long run.

Stage One: Attraction: This is the early stage where you are focused on fun and optimism, seeing multiple men, being the girl, and letting them court and provide for you. It's the time to keep things light, with lots of breathing space for you and chasing space for him.

Stage Two: Uncertainty: After seeing a number of men, you begin to feel like you may have found someone that you would like to see exclusively. Doubts come up. One or both parties may pull away a bit. It is a time to know that the uncertainty about someone may mean they are actually a real candidate, and not the opposite.

Stage Three: Exclusivity: This lovely period is about doing exactly what you did in stage one with one person instead of several. It is not yet the time for deep emotional dives or full sexual intimacy. You are not "in relationship." You are still *in courtship* with one man.

Stage Four: Intimacy: After enjoying dating one person exclusively for a while, the deeper connections start to occur, emotionally and physically. Some role reversal may occur. Probably still not the time for full sexual intimacy if you want to be headed toward marriage.

Stage Five: Engagement: He's proposed. This is a vital stage in the maturation of your relationship where you both practice different skills that will be necessary in marriage. You're negotiating lifestyle and more personal, intimate issues. You are "trying on" what it might be like to be married, and seeing if you want to move forward into a lifetime commitment. If you are not interested in marriage, perhaps it's a stage where you live together and blend your lives.

A lot of women jump from stage one to stage four, or skip one, two, and three altogether. That behavior is a set up for over-investment, followed by disillusionment and disappointment for both parties. So understanding the stages and navigating them in order will probably be new for you. Hang in there, and see what kind of results occur if you lay a firm foundation.

13

Looking for a Date Rather Than a Mate

If everything was cool, and you were comfortable receiving from a generous, cherishing man, and you didn't feel like you needed to prove to him why *he* should choose *you*, and, whether or not there was chemistry, you could date slowly and keep your head, and easily see several men simultaneously... *If* your self-worth was profoundly intact, and it was not dependent on your ability to give and take care of others, and *if* you clearly understood the stages of dating, and could navigate them gracefully and consistently, and *if* your ability to spot self-centered or narcissistic men up front was consistent and keen... Then I would say only date men who are potential mates.

But if those "ifs'" don't exist for you, you need to get used to dating men who treat you well, and with whom you *don't* have a lot of chemistry. Think of it as field research where you are studying different kinds of men as they interact romantically, as well as studying yourself in the same situations.

So you need to practice, right? The old game of "get out there and find the right guy and get into some size, fast," is no longer on the table. The new game is: date a lot of men with whom you have a minimal investment, and learn how to exercise these new skill sets until you're confident and competent as a feminine energy woman. Your entry point is, "How is he treating me, how do I feel in his presence, and is it my best guess that he's a masculine man?" No longer are you looking for compatibility and chemistry up front. In fact, too much of either might be a detriment. Instead you are focusing on his ability to court and cherish you.

If he passes through those initial assessments, and you like him 51%, get dressed up and go have a good time. Date until it's fun. Go for lots of experiences with different men while you develop new habits and new perspectives. When you are constantly maintaining your feminine position, and your dating skills are strong, you will be able to see men with whom you share more chemistry and compatibility without losing your head.

In this new process you will probably encounter a couple of significant challenges, based on false assumptions.

Challenge #1: *I'm leading him on if I let him take me out when I know, up front, that he's not relationship material.*

The false assumption that underlies this challenge is that men think about dating like women think about dating.

Most masculine men go on a date to have fun, show you a good time, and to enjoy the company of a beautiful, happy woman. In other words, they ask you out for the purpose of *having a successful date.* Unlike most women, who use a date to begin the process of "relating" in service to eventually building a relationship, these guys have a complete experience with you, starting with picking you up or meeting at the designated dating site, and ending with saying good night or goodbye. Then they go home and think about the date, what was said and what happened between you, and they decide whether or not they want to see you for another date. It's harder for them to think and feel at the same time, so they feel a lot when they're with you, and think later.

Women will frequently be "trying on" a man while they're on a first date: thinking about various aspects of their future life and inserting him into those aspects, e.g., *"would my parents like him, can I imagine him meeting my friends, what would he be like to travel with, can I imagine kissing him, would we like the same kind of interior design?"* etc., etc., etc. We are auditioning him for our future while he is just having a good time in a restaurant with a beautiful woman who is wearing pretty colors, laughs easily, and seems to be enjoying the food.

Challenge #2: *It's unfair for me to let him pay for me when I'm not that serious about him.*

The false assumption here is that men think about money and giving the same way that women think about money and giving.

Masculine men are fulfilled when they give, provide, protect, and cherish. They also fall in love when they give. As long as they feel appreciated and respected, and have the experience of hitting the target through their giving, they're happy. (Hitting the target, in this case, means clearly understanding that what they provided increased your happiness, comfort, or safety.)

Because masculine men are looking for a date rather than a mate in stage one dating, they are investing their cash in hopes of having a great date, and watching you thoroughly enjoy yourself. A man usually does his initial culling before the date – in other words, before he asks you out he will have assessed whether or not he thinks there might be some long-term potential with you, if he wants long-term potential. Sometimes a man just wants an enjoyable evening making a beautiful woman happy. He might go home after that enjoyable evening and decide that he wants to do it again, and maybe next time he'll want to have an enjoyable evening making a beautiful woman wearing an evening gown happy, so it's the opera and a five-star restaurant. One of the reasons that masculine men make money is so they can spend some of it making women happy. It's kind of a hobby, like golf or fishing or collecting antique automobiles. I'm not saying that women are toys or trophies to these guys. I'm saying that masculine men enjoy having fun, and enjoy having *large* fun, and they don't generally get heavy and deep fast. They feel really good about that game of golf if the course is beautiful and challenging, and they have nice gear. They have a fun day in their new, cool boat trying out the new rod, and bagging the big one. And a night of taking her out to a nice place, and she looks gorgeous, and enjoys herself, and smiles, and is warm and confident...

Well, that was worth the output.

Case closed.

14

How Good Can It Get?

My favorite phone calls from female clients are the ones where they've really experienced, often for the first time, the attention and cherishing of a masculine man. There's an amazement in their voices, coupled with exclamations such as, *"I had no idea!" "I can't believe this!" "What have I been doing all of my life with men up to now?!"*

I find that many women have limited ideas about what they need, and about what is actually *possible* in romantic relationships. They are particularly clueless about what courtship is, and how beneficial, and delightful, and nourishing it is. Most women seem to have the idea that dating is a drag, and they want to avoid it: just find the right guy and get into a stage four relationship (committed intimacy) as quickly as possible. And, because they have no real idea about what a generous, cherishing man can offer them, they hang out in looking for chemistry and compatibility, thinking, *"If the guy is cute and we like the same things, I'm good."*

Ouch.

This brave philosophy assures that such women's romantic lives will probably be dominated by "trying" – trying to find the right guy, trying to be the women that she thinks he wants her to be, trying to reconcile the eventual emptiness in her soul with thoughts like, *"We have so much in common,"* or *"He's really a nice guy,"* or *"He's so handsome and we're both Buddhists, and you can't have everything, right?"*

Have you heard anything like this coming out of your mouth before?

Meanwhile, there is an entire class of men that these women don't even *see* – men who live for the joy of studying and providing for their pleasure, comfort, and safety. And why don't women see these guys?

Because the chemistry/compatibility lens through which they're surveying the romantic terrain is actually *filtering those men out* most of the time. This is not to say that you can't, or won't, have chemistry and compatibility with your prince. But when your primary criteria for deciding who is good for you shifts to how a man treats you, and whether he is generous and cherishing, *the whole experience of what chemistry and compatibility means also shifts.*

I have a client who had her second date with a generous, cherishing man recently. She was only willing to go on a first date because we surveyed his profile online together, and assessed that he was treating her well in his initial emails. She was quite sure that there was absolutely no physical attraction, and it was in question whether or not their lifestyles and interests were aligned enough to even make him worth a conversation over coffee. But, because she is practicing the art of looking for a date rather than looking for a mate, and learning how to develop a healthy relationship in the meantime, she was willing to give him a shot. After the first date, she was considering cutting him loose, but he was still treating her very well. So I encouraged her to have a second date.

Somehow, on that second date, as he continued to provide for her in a beautiful manner, something changed. And at the end of the date, there was a little smooching, and then he said, *"If we continue to see each other I would like to take you to bed."* Although she reiterated that his looks didn't particularly appeal to her when we spoke after that second date, she said that, for some reason, it just didn't matter what he looked like, and that it felt really good to kiss him and to hear him say the bed remark. And when she thought about those things later, she got turned on. Her voice was light and her feminine energy was clearly relaxed and centered. It was beautiful. She is moving very slowly through the dating process, and, wisely, has three or four guys in play simultaneously. All of this allows her to keep her investment in each man fairly low, and to stay centered in her own breathing space so she can really tell how she feels and what she wants. She may or may not see this guy again. But she is allowing herself to be impacted by his masculine energy and attention, and that is providing her with a new, and very wonderful experience.

So, if my client had eliminated Mr. X on the grounds of chemistry and compatibility up front, she would have robbed herself of this surprising and pleasurable exchange. She was actually building neurological muscle memory for being receptively feminine. And, more to the point, her concept of chemistry and compatibility changed with him, quite naturally, in the sunshine of his very masculine attentions. Her experience with him was really nice, and she was turned on gently, safely, and unexpectedly.

Really good.

15

Criteria vs. Qualifications: The Courtship Thing

We have criteria and we have qualifications. In the realm of online dating, there are two lists – one list of must haves from your potential dates, and one list of what it is you can offer this potential date that would be attractive to him.

- I call the list of what it takes for you to consider someone as a potential date "criteria," e.g., you need a man who will treat you well, knows how to fulfill himself in his business, is financially solvent, loves to give, is generous and courageous, etc.
- I call the list of what you are offering in order to have someone consider *you* as a potential date "qualifications," e.g., I am joyful, sensuous, optimistic, etc.

So here's the deal: most women believe that *we* are the ones who have to convince *men* that we're worthy of being chosen *by men* as potential dates. We feel like we need to focus on *his* criteria and try and be what he wants. After all, we're used to selling ourselves out there in the real world, and that's worked pretty well so far. So we just transfer that skill set to the internet and watch the magic happen, right?

How's it goin' so far?

The problem is that it's actually the job of the feminine to *be* courted, rather than being the one *to do* the courting. And when we're using our energy to try and get men to like us, we become the pursuer.

Let's look at Webster's definition of "court":

1. To pay attention to (a person) in order to get something.
2. To try and get the love of; woo.
3. To seek; as, to court favor.

Let's check out "woo" while we're at it:
1. To make love to or seek to marry.
2. To seek; as, she *wooed* fame.
3. To coax. *v.i.* to woo a person. – woo'er, *n.*

Okay... So courtship is about somebody (the woo'er) paying attention to somebody else (the woo'ee) to try and get her love and favor for the purpose of making love to, and/or marrying her.

Holy Retroactive Grand-Maternal Advice, Batgirl!

There's a whole thing here that we're wired to want, and often educated to condemn.

That can't be right.

We know we want a man who is financially viable, a great, courageous communicator, a man who exudes juicy chemistry, has done his personal work so that he brings a whole healthy man to the mix, has balance, shared values, high integrity, optimism, great friends, a fabulous castle, and plenty of time to give to The Relationship. We want his respect and support for our path in life.

No argument there.

However, it's the other hard-wired thing that needs addressing, because without it, we get a friend and a partner with benefits, but we don't get the deep dive into our own feminine nature that we must have in order to live in the field of satisfied grace.

And that other thing is to be courted. We want courtship, mostly, *really.* We want a man who is strong, and generous, and courageous, and funny, and together, who's ridin' around on his steed doing good deeds, and feeling confident and self-assured. We want that man to look at us and be struck lovesick, lovesick in a way that renders him vital, and energized and creative. We want him to feel like we're his ultimate "it" girl, and we want him to want us, and pursue us, and bring us flowers and gifts with his masculine edge securely intact. We crave the experience of having him worship the ground we walk on, and watching him work for the privilege of being able to put his spun gold cape across the mud so we can walk on it without getting our dainty little feet dirty on a rainy day.

Guaranteed.

So part of our new job is to be clear about our criteria for the men we want to meet, *focus on his qualifications,* and to learn how to vet potential suitors to see if *they've* got what *we* need. Later we'll look at how to do that in a manner that is clear and methodical. There's a whole new sense of power, dignity, and confidence that comes with this perspective.

16

How Online Dating Helps

If you keep doing what you've always done, you'll get what you've always gotten.

Let's say that throughout your 20s and 30s you worked as a ranger for the forest service, and you cleared trails, took care of campgrounds, tended to the ecology, and got a monthly paycheck. If you had never run a business, and never had any business education, and you decided to leave your job with the forest service and become a party planner, what might happen?

Because you've never created and sustained a prosperous business, after a year the business flops. You then decide to try and become an importer of rare artifacts from the Far East. If, after a year, *tha*t business flopped, chances are that somewhere along the line you might realize that the silver bullet is not finding the right kind of business, but, instead, *learning how to run a successful business.*

This metaphor applies to dating successfully for the purpose of meeting a great guy and becoming involved in a fulfilling long-term relationship. The "I should just know how to do this," and "Other women can do it and so can I" school of bombarding the romantic arena in your life with good intentions, strategies that work elsewhere in your life, and best guesses has probably taken you to the mat a number of times.

Just like non-business women who want to become successful in business generally need education, mentoring, models, and practice, those of us who didn't receive healthy romantic educations also need new information, mentoring, models, and practice. I find that starting from a basecamp of beginner's mind, with a stance of teachability, reaps the most solid and dependable rewards.

I like online dating as a context for the learning process because it is a contained medium where you can meet men who are there to be met. You get a lot of pertinent info up front, like his marital status, kids, faith, education, lifestyle, habits, and age, and you can remain anonymous as you go. You are in charge of the speed of your interactions, and you can freeze-frame the process at any time. It is a petri dish where you can observe yourself, your thoughts, habits, actions, and responses, and where you can keep a cool head as you find out who these men are.

Oxytocin is the bonding chemical that is released by the brain when we hit a certain point of feel-good or intimacy with someone (we'll talk more about this later), and when it's released, one of its primary purposes is procreation. It begins to blur what is not pleasing about our potential mate, and it boosts our reaction to the good stuff. It's a great high as long as you've had a chance to thoroughly vet your guy before oxytocin kicks in. Otherwise you end up bonding too soon, having the problems get blurry, go for the deep dive, invest too soon, and then come up for air in six months to find out that you're with someone who you don't like, or with whom you are not compatible.

If that deep, inadequately vetted dive occurs, what ensues can be a nasty little dance where you either try and change those things in him that you don't like, or you try and modify your own needs and feelings because you're already "in" and this is "the guy." Women who do the early oxytocin dance often become the women who habitually talk a lot about how much compromise is required in romance, the "*Well, you can't have everything*" gals. Not that romantic relationships don't require compromise, and maybe you can't always have *everything* (although I know women who say they actually *do* have everything they want). But when you take the time to *slowly* learn who a man is before substantially bonding through spending too much time, too quickly, too many deep emotional dives, or the premature sharing of bodily fluids, you can actually choose to bond with men who are likely to bring a lot more of what you want and need to the table, and with whom you will negotiate far less.

Go figure…

17

What Happened to Men
and How Women Lead

"So, Sierra, where are these guys, this mythical tribe of he-men who allegedly live for the satisfaction for "providing, protecting, and cherishing" their women. Cause I'm not seein' 'em. I'm seein' guys who either fawn all over me and lose their power and masculinity when they do it, or I'm seein' the ones who want what they want when they want it, no matter how I feel about it. Neither of these kinds of men are acceptable reasons for shaving my legs and wasting a night at some Indian dive when I could be home, relaxing in my PJ's, and watching 'The Thomas Crown Affair,' again, with my galpals."

Understandable sentiments – unnecessary, but understandable. I am not a therapist, nor am I a sociologist. But, from years of coaching and learning, I know what I know, and one of the things that I know is that, for quite a while, courtship was one of the casualties of the women's movement. For sure, we all needed a redefinition of women's power, self-esteem, market value, and capabilities. No argument there. And with that redefinition, it was critical to deconstruct gender roles, and explore and experiment with all forms of equality, reciprocity, and power structures. Had to be done. And aren't we, as women, all stronger, more autonomous, more self-loving, more self-generating, and more visionary because of those battles fought and won?

No question.

But the guys... Let's talk about the guys. They became the villains to many women, and at least highly suspect to others. Not that there weren't, and aren't, morally questionable men out there. And, of course, after a cultural history skewed by patriarchal values, it's no wonder that women, as a gender, needed to unleash Kali, the destroyer, and express and enact all of that generational rage on men, as a gender. Yep. That was a karmic debt that had to be paid. And it ain't over yet. But the lion's share of western women's redefinition has been significantly put in motion.

Meanwhile men were put through the cosmic Cuisinart, and came out the other side fairly confused about their manhood, and what that was, and what that meant, especially in terms of romance. Is it sexist to open the car door for a woman, or be turned on by her beauty, or want to provide for her comfort? What's neurosis and what's instinctive? What's nature and what's nurture? My experience is that men actually don't feel very good about themselves, or women, when they're focused on organizing their lives around the pursuit of their own pleasure, a.k.a. narcissistic. Yet their masculine instincts have often been fairly wounded, so they're sometimes confused, self-focused, and/or awkward. I'm grateful that teachers and movements that help men redefine and integrate the healthy masculine have surfaced in recent decades. I love men, I need men, and I honor the difficulty of their path in the last 70 years.

So here we women are, capable, autonomous, and pretty darn lonely for something that's hard to even name because it was a baby that got thrown out with the feminist bathwater. And here the guys are, working their way back to what they need to be in order to feel right with themselves, and the women they interact with. And courtship is one of the common denominators in this reach toward one another.

Here's the thing: as we've talked about previously, most women are so used to assessing whether men are "right" for them through the lenses of chemistry and compatibility (*"Is he cute and do we like the same things?"*), that they don't even know how to conceptualize, much less recognize, much less attract and encourage, chivalrous, courting men. And, since capable women often move into the mode of selling themselves to men, there's a platform for interaction, romantically, that often doesn't happen.

Here's what that platform looks and acts like: a woman focuses first and foremost on how a man is treating her. Is he enthusiastic? Does he compliment her? Does he ask questions? Women need to check out his masculinity, not their compatibility or chemistry, first.

Masculine men come forward in that masculinity when it is responded to, and received by, the women that they're pursuing. The masculine men you're looking for are looking for you. You'll recognize them by how they treat you, and you'll reveal and amplify the wonderfulness of their courtship by the way you recognize and receive it. Just as women become exhausted by trying to get men to like them, by "overgiving" and by trying to sell themselves, men get complacent and self-centered when their impulses to give are not received, and, instead, they are either unrecognized, reciprocated, or blocked. So the guys you're looking for are often right in front of you, but you can't recognize them because your focus is elsewhere, and that elsewhere *actually encourages narcissism*. In other words, out of ignorance and assumption, we encourage men to be more feminine, and then we get pissed off and disappointed when they respond to that encouragement.

I'm not saying that women are solely responsible for the way that men think and behave. Nor am I saying that there aren't some rotten apples in the barrel. But I am saying that we have an enormous amount of influence over how we're treated, and what kind of dynamics are created and stabilized in our romantic lives. Our ability to recognize who men are, and to bring out the best in them in a feminine-forward manner is one of the ways in which women lead.

18

An End to Indictment

It's amazing to me how quickly some women can make hostile or defensive assumptions about men. In the face of limited information, a guilty-until-proven-innocent stance is taken. Everything from name-calling (*idiot, sleazeball, predator, pervert*), to harsh judgments (*"He's just in it for sex," "He's clearly a player"*), to questioning his motives (*"Why would he say that?" "Why would he contact me when we're 500 miles from each other?"*).

Often there's a dismissive or critical tone in a woman's voice when she tells me how he's out of the running, or that she would never even consider him. It's an ugly, bitter quality that bleeds through.

It's not that there aren't some questionable guys out there. But I find that on legitimate dating sites where people are mainly looking for relationships or love, the majority of men are pretty goodhearted, and often clueless. They may be awkward or confused. Usually narcissistic or just plain mean men will make it pretty obvious up front who they are, and a lot of the work in this book helps you recognize those announcements.

But the rest of the men, whether you like them or not, are good guys who really want to find a woman they can love. Isn't that wonderful?

We can go online and see thousands of men who are basically wearing their hearts on their sleeves because they want to love and be loved. It's a risk every time they reach out to a woman, and they probably have to get used to a lot of rejection.

So I want to encourage you to drop your sword and shield, and soften a little when you see them. Try and appreciate their courage and intentions. Try and assume the best about them. You don't have to respond to them or interact with them. And I'm not asking you to take care of their feelings. I'm simply suggesting that you try thinking well of men, for the sake of your own heart and spirit.

I love them. I love the craggy-faced sailor who is 75 and lives on his boat, who sends me a note to tell me that I'm beautiful and could he take me out for coffee sometime? I love the 27-year-old Latin hunk who contacts me to tell me that I look really sexy and would I be interested in having some fun with a younger man? I love the lonely guy from Klamath Falls who lost his wife to cancer last year and thinks we have a lot in common.

I like being told I'm beautiful, or smart, or desirable. I like being asked out. I'm anonymous online. I am safe. There is no demand on me. So I put a mantle of kindness over my thoughts and interactions with men. It's good for my soul. I suggest you try on this idea.

19

Women Teach Men How to Treat Them

That's a fact. From the very first interaction we let these guy know who we are, and how we expect to be treated. It shows up in many ways. We'll get into the specifics of it as we get into the specifics of the information and skill sets in this book.

But, for now, I'd like to impress this truth upon you. You are in charge of who gets in the gate, and your understanding of men and the dynamics of courtship are the basecamp for making sure that you are clearly setting the bar where you want it.

20

The Dance of Conscious Courtship

If you regard what you are learning here as a new form of dance, I believe that metaphor may make this an easier and more enjoyable process. If you were taking tango lessons, let's say, you would know, up front, that you'd be in for a playful, partner-oriented, sensual ride. If you weren't a particularly skilled or experienced dancer, you would probably also know that you would be exercising beginner's mind, making a lot of mistakes, and that you would probably be there to enjoy being moved around the dance floor by men for the purpose of learning and playing. You would be practicing a new language, a movement vocabulary, composed of unfamiliar ways to hold your arms and torso, and extend your neck, and intertwine your legs with his, and sexy attitudes, and following his lead: all kinds of complex and beautiful new ways to ultimately create a synergy with a man that is fun, and feminine, and *initially foreign*. You'd probably wear pretty dresses or skirts, and dancer's high heels, and, the more you got into it, the more you would show up as the woman that you are. In some partner classes, you dance with many men, so you're constantly moving from the arms of one guy to the next. Chances are you would laugh easily, and let your hair down, and that the mistakes would be just as joyful as the mastery.

So, as much as you can, I invite you to adopt this *"I'm here to learn and play"* attitude as we move forward in the dating domain: the less perfectionism and impatience, the better. This is a significant undertaking, so let's infuse it with as much discovery, adventure, and fun as possible.

21

Speaking of the "F" Word

Fun… Dating is about having fun, initially. The beginning stages are a time for joy and optimism and, well, fun.

Good to remember.

22

Watching Him Increase Your Pleasure

Masculine men will study your happiness and pleasure, and then organize themselves and their resources around providing and increasing those things for you. Once they are, in Alison Armstrong's words, "charmed and enchanted" by you, they are compelled to "provide, protect, and cherish." I said *compelled*. So when women begin to attract, recognize, and be courted by masculine men, these are the kinds of comments I hear:

"I've never had a man treat me like this."

"He really listened to what I said I liked, and then he remembered later."

"Oh my God! Oh my God! I had no idea."

Something else to take note of is that, generally, when women are dating masculine men, they (the women) feel confident, relaxed, and happy. Even if he's not "the one," his attention and open-hearted courtship will allow you to be in your power and yumminess with no hint of fear that you're not doing it right, or that he's judging you. And, conversely, I find that when there's a more narcissistic man on board, women feel insecure, distracted, anxious, and/or uncomfortable. Your feelings are a pretty clear litmus test for what kind of man you're seeing.

23

How It Feels When You Get Your Energy Back

Good. That's how it feels.

As women begin to allow themselves to be courted and cherished, they discover an energetic setpoint that is about relaxing at the center of their being. There is a way in which most high-performance women are constantly "at attention" on a core level: alert, outwardly-focused, ready to anticipate, accommodate, articulate, and handle whatever comes at them. We are actually designed to be fluid, and this adaptive rigidity takes a lot to sustain. I remember a male client of mine speaking about a first date he had with a woman who was an executive coach. He said it was uncomfortable for him because she sat straight up in her chair, and even leaned a little forward, the whole time they were together. She never relaxed.

As I've mentioned previously, women can become exhausted, deep down inside, from so much vigilance. So it may feel a bit unfamiliar, initially, to not be on high watch all the time. But very quickly I find that the relief of having a man around who wants to handle things, and is capable of doing so, is an invitation for women to really let go. That kind of nervous system surrender supports and induces more sensuality, pleasure, self-love, and energy. It also begins to feel very natural. I would call it a neurological *remembering*, and it can infuse a woman's entire walk in this world. We start to engage organic magnetism, rather than effort, as a neurological baseline. The right men support us in re-establishing this base of magnetism as the primary MO for how we live and create, and they recharge us and strengthen that magnetism within us, in an ongoing way. It's a perfect energetic ecology: they are energized by providing for our happiness, and we are energized by receiving their provision.

It's good.

It's really, *really* good.

24

Success Watermark #1

Good work! So far you have read about, and begun to assimilate, a lot of new perspectives and understandings. You have done some self-reflection. You have been willing to challenge your old thinking. You have probably sat through some uncomfortable feelings, and become willing to go to the next level with the process.

This thing takes patience, courage, and vulnerability. Take a moment to breathe and celebrate all of that.

PART 2:

The Online Process: Let's Get This Party Started!

Okay here we go!

As we're moving into the "how to" of this dance, I want to give you a quick reminder of where we're going, and why, because this part of the book is where habit collides with new behavior. You may have been doing things differently than suggested here for a long time. Consequently, you may be somewhat reactive as I coach you into a more feminine mode. I encourage you to pace yourself, acknowledge any feelings that may come up as you try the new tools, and check in with your buddy. Give this process a shot, remembering that the golden ring is a man who adores and courts you without losing his edge, and who will continue to adore and court you for the duration of your relationship.

25

The Three Types of Cyber Suitors

Let's clearly identify the kinds of men that you will encounter as you begin to open online profiles and interact with potential cyber-suitors.

The three types of men are:

> *A. Masculine men (MMs)*
> *B. Narcissistic men (NATs)*
> *(I am referring to men who are excessively self-centered, and not necessarily pathologically narcissistic)*
> *C. Masculine men who behave somewhat complacently (MATs)*

A. Masculine men (MMs): Happy, optimistic, generous, playful, self-fulfilled, high self-esteem, protecting, providing, cherishing, high integrity. They are the gold standard.

A masculine man will be interested in finding out whether or not:

- You like him
- You are interested in having him pursue you
- You are a woman who he could make happy
- You are able to let him lead and give him chasing space
- You have time for him
- You know how to receive what he wants to give, with joyous receptivity
- You are optimistic and playful

B. Self-centered or narcissistic men (NATs): Moody, emotionally seductive, vain, mixed messages, shaky self-esteem, concerned with enlisting and controlling you, want *you* to provide for *them*. Often they are rich, attractive, and/or powerful guys. Not so good.

A narcissistic man will be interested in finding out whether or not:

- *He* likes *you*
- You're willing to pursue *him*
- You are a woman who could make *him* happy
- He can control you into chasing *him*
- He wants to give you any time
- He'll like what you give *him*
- You care more about *his* feelings than your own

C. Masculine men who are presenting somewhat complacently because women have done too much for them (MATs):

Masculine men who behave more complacently will be interested in finding out whether or not:

- You will see who he actually is, and behave accordingly
- You will make him take the lead
- You will volunteer information he hasn't asked for
- You will engage with his potential negativity or over-disclosure
- You will reciprocate

These men have had women do too much for them, possibly because they are very attractive, powerful, or wealthy. They are hoping to find a woman who will operate from her femininity and self-love with them, and call them out as the masculine man that they are. When they find and interact with such women, sometimes they grumble a little bit at first, and then they blossom into beautiful masculine men who are vital, loving, and very creative about studying your pleasure and well-being. Bonus points.

As we move into decrypting emails and profiles, I will be talking mainly about how MMs and NATs present themselves. MATs will be a combination of the two. So if you encounter men who are combining the pictures, wording, and approaches of both, check your gut. If you feel relaxed as you read the correspondence or profiles of these guys, proceed as though they are masculine and see what happens.

26

Receiving Does Not Signal Reciprocity

If you've dated NATs before, you learned that *everything they gave came with a price.* And that taught you to be very careful about accepting what they offered. That's the way it goes with those men.

However, masculine men groove on giving. And what they want to receive in exchange is your enjoyment of, and appreciation for, what was given. Later, as you move into more sustained dating with such a man, there will be times when you provide for him: a nice home-cooked dinner, tickets to an event you know he'd like, a picnic and a plan for a Sunday outing. But not until later, and not nearly to the degree that he gives. His main instinct is to give for the purpose of increasing your pleasure and well-being, and that will remain a prominent dynamic in your time together, forever, as long as *he* keeps receiving *your* increased appreciation and illumination in response. So learning to relax and receive without the demand for reciprocity is a new skill that is fun and necessary to practice. It's a simple concept to understand, and a big shift to implement for many of my clients. Women who have mastered the art of being in charge of their lives need to learn to turn that piece off when dating. The masculine/feminine arrangement in early dating is that the man gives and the woman just receives. Try it on and see how it feels.

I think you'll like it.

27

The Dating Profile: General Profile Guidelines

Online dating provides a unique opportunity to attract, and interact with, many different kinds of men. So let's talk about the elements of a profile, and delve into the specific how-to's.

As we begin this journey, here are a few reminders and over-arching principles to keep in mind:

Principles that Apply Specifically to Online Profiles and Pics

As you are learning, masculine men are a wonderful breed of inherently good, tender, generous, playful, loyal, and creative creatures. They are very visual, and are attracted to beauty, joy, warmth, kindness, and color. It is important for them to feel that it is safe to approach you, and they often look to your eyes and smile for clues. When they see a woman in a pretty skirt or dress, they feel excited and appreciative. Skin is very sexy to them: it insinuates accessibility, and shows that you're open and willing to be touched, when the time is right. It is also an indicator of energy and vitality. Driven by a desire to make you happy, these men want to know that you are available, optimistic, and playful, and that you are a woman who will allow and enjoy their lead. Initially brevity is often attractive to them. They are motivated to pursue when they are given enough chasing space. They deeply need to be liked as they are, and they thrive on respect.

MMs will *lead* the dating process: they will take your number, ask you out, arrange the date, make reservations, pick you up, and pay for the date. Then they'll follow up and create the next date if that's what you both want. They will plan, provide, and implement, based on your pleasure. This is an important principle to understand. You may have never experienced dating a man with a strong lead before. As we go along, you'll be learning how to recognize, accept, and encourage that lead in a manner that allows you to feel comfortable and relaxed. Don't worry about it right now. Just know that you can look forward to this kind of courtship.

28

He'll Read Your Profile Like a Job Description

So, onto the process.

Your profile and pics are a job description to masculine men, a job that they're looking for. And that job is: find a woman to whom I'm attracted, who is available for, and receptive to, my protection, provision, and cherishing.

That would be you.

So the way your profile is constructed and the particular qualities displayed in your photos will allow him to clearly understand the job at hand, and whether or not he is a good candidate for it. He will be looking for a woman with whom he can play, and for whom he can provide, and who, in turn, will have time for him. He wants a woman who knows how to enjoy life, gauge her own comfort and enjoyment, and who knows how to, and likes to, receive graciously. He doesn't want to compete with her busy schedule, or compete for the lead. And he needs a woman who loves herself more than she will ever love him.

Photos

This is a fairly big subject, so I will mention it here and then go into greater detail in an upcoming chapter.

As we've talked about, a guy is very visual, and when your photos speak to your beauty, spirit, and receptivity, he will come in the door. You are the job, and your photos are the job title: "Happy, warm, beautiful, self-loving woman available for cherishing."

Ahhh... That's his expertise, so he reads on.

Your Username, Byline, and Geographic Radius

All of these elements add to his sense that he's looking at an appropriate job for his talents – a username that is feminine, and allows him to know what to call you, a byline that advertises qualities that are important to the success of his work, and a wide enough geographic radius that it alludes to some openness and breathing space on your part.

I'm a big fan of creating usernames that include an endearment of some kind that infers that you're beautiful, e.g., belle_espirit, or jolie_amie. Italian and French usernames seem to do the trick, and they may attract men who are a little more cultured or sophisticated. You can also use a name that *feels* beautiful and feminine, and clearly lets him know what to call you. It can be a word that describes something beautiful, e.g., Jade_Dreams, Summer, LilyRose, Rain, or a name that sounds soft and beautiful, e.g., Kiah, Anasuya. For a while you will sign your emails to him using some part of your username, such as "belle," and he will call you by that name. He becomes accustomed to calling you some form of "beautiful," and it actually sets up a dynamic of cherishing immediately. You can use your instincts and imagination here. Maybe you want to be called "dear" – "Cara." Maybe it would feel good to be referred to as "Joy" or "Grace." The point is that women teach men how to treat them, and this is the beginning of his education that you are a woman who he will regard with affection, admiration, and cherishing.

Sometimes women create usernames that do not let a man know how to address her, like "FLJen2022" or "Skydancing." The first example is fairly asexual, and the second would be a nice subtitle, but doesn't really give him a handle on what to call you. So the principle is to be aware that you're creating a name that he will identify with you, and with which he can express his regard for you, and choose accordingly.

I'm also a big fan of a period of anonymity in the early email exchanges. So, by having a username that insinuates an endearment, which he will use for a while, he gets a little mystery and chasing space, while practicing an act of cherishing. Good for everyone.

As far as subtitles go, I suggest that you think about essence qualities that would describe you if you were a fragrance or a taste. One of my clients used, *"Classic with a spicy kick."* Sometimes listing adjectives that you feel describe you, and then choosing, say, three of them as a subtitle works well, especially when you have a handle on what masculine men will be looking for. In short, he's looking for a woman who is joyful, playful, relaxed, adventurous, authentic, sensual, optimistic, receptive, happy, laughs easily, has time for him, enjoys life, is effervescent, passionate, has strong values, loves herself, takes excellent care of herself, and is not afraid to be beautiful. Overall, he is looking for announcements in your profile that you are an open, available, attractive, and happy woman who will be receptive to his gifts and pleasuring, and that you are a woman who responds to the world with enthusiasm, joy, and appreciation. List some adjectives that describe you. Cull through them and choose the ones that fall into the above categories, and try using a few as your subtitle: *"Peaceful, playful, adventurous,"* or *"Sassy, sensual, and joyful."*

Another way to approach subtitles is to use a simple, optimistic phrase that gives him a sense of your response to life such as, "Life is so beautiful," or "Each day a new adventure." Sometimes women are so jaded that they feel that showing their softer sense of well-being is "cheesy" or "clichéd." I find that these are generally women who are accustomed to choosing and pursuing narcissistic men. Those men want to be entertained by your wit. Masculine men just want to know that you're happy and can be made even happier by them. I've read a lot of subtitles where women are subtly (or not so subtly) telling men what to do, such as, *"Let's make dreams together,"* or *"Come fly away with me."* Usually masculine men don't want to be told what to do. The message may be soft, but MMs see it and feel it.

So far so good.

The Nuts and Bolts of Your Text

I will describe the purpose and feeling of your text. The profile questions following this section will help you glean the information necessary to construct a profile that follows these guidelines. After the questions is a sample profile that will give you a template from which to work.

A couple of general guidelines: MMs respond to brevity, so you can keep it shorter and to the point. Also, put a space between your paragraphs. He will actually visually register that formatted space as *you* being more spacious.

Your first paragraph will further reinforce what your photos inferred: indeed, you are a happy, life-loving woman who knows herself, and is open to being impacted by what he brings to the dance – more good and more joy.

Cool.

The second paragraph gets down to some foundational aspects of the possible longevity of this position: your values, character, moral fiber, what inspires you, and what you stand for. He can see that you know yourself, and that you are a woman of substance.

Paragraph three addresses what kind of man you respect. Remember that he thrives when his character is respected, just as you thrive when you are cherished. Two or three sentences about the kind of man you respect works.

(Note: Masculine men are honest and reliable. A lot of times women who have been with self-centered men state that they respect men who are honest and reliable. It's okay to state those qualities, but it tends toward projection.)

Fourth paragraph: Once he sees that you respect men like him, he's interested in knowing if you will be attracted to him. So several sentences on that subject will tell the tale. Focus on inner qualities rather than physical features. Caveat: Some women really need to be with a man who possesses certain physical characteristics, i.e., who is taller than they are, or has a certain build or athleticism. If you are one of those women, this would be a good place to mention it.

Fifth paragraph: What kind of men cause you to feel comfortable and relaxed?

And, lastly, the sixth paragraph lets him know what you find sexy. Keep it classy and maybe a little flirtatious. Masculine men pay big attention to this information.

In reference to men reading your profile as a job description, I wanted to include this actual email from a gentleman to one of my clients after seeing her profile. The quotes are the excerpts from her text followed by his comments in bold. This guy is a garden variety MM. Her user name is Daphne.

"I respect men who are kind, responsible, and adept at self-assessment and self-reflection. I look up to men who enjoy being deeply engaged with life." **CHECK**

"I am attracted to men who are confident and competent, men who are genuinely interested in others and who are emotionally fluent." **CHECK**

"I am comfortable with men who are team players. It's wonderful to be next to a man who has my back with a centered and gentle strength." **CHECK**

"I like a man with a plan. Empathy and humor are sexy to me." **CHECK**

"Daphne
I read your profile…see above…
Cheers
Jack"

I love these guys so much.

If you choose to go with Match.com as your base camp dating site, you will also want to think about the following categories. All three of the next sections will provide him with information about how to court you. Very practical.

For fun: Keep the categories general – movies, cultural events, farmers' markets, getaways to the coast, hiking, etc. Let him come up with specifics.

Favorite hotspots: Same principles apply – anything from types of travel destinations to specific categories of dating venues.

Favorite things: What can he give to you? – chocolate, flowers, the New York Times, being served breakfast in bed, watching wild horses, the sound of the wind in the pines, etc.

Here are some suggestions to jog your choices.

Some ideas for fun:
Movies
Theater
Cooking together
Opera
Eco-adventures
Comedy clubs
Restaurants
Sports with others
Hiking
Camping
Partner dancing
Biking
Bookstores
Kayaking
Farmers' markets

Taking a fun new class
Being on or near large natural bodies of water
Kicking around charming little towns
Spontaneous getaways
Day trips
Yoga retreats
Cruises

Some hotspot choices:
The tropics
Warm beaches
Cold, foggy coastlines
Jazz clubs
Lush forests
Sophisticated cities
Farm-to-table dining
Little bed & breakfasts
Big outdoor concert venues
Rivers

Some favorite things:
Fresh flowers
A warm fire in the fireplace on rainy days
Favorite hot drinks
A surprise picnic
The sound of the sea
Cooking together
French perfume
The smell of pines
Beautiful lace

29

Profile Questions

These questions will mine and uncover the basic information necessary to create a profile designed to attract generous, cherishing men. You will use your answers to present your essence in language that will draw him toward you.

1. List some of the optimistic qualities that describe you, e.g., playful, joyful, intuitive, etc. What makes you happy? What lights you up? What relaxes you? What causes you to feel inspired?

2. What do you value in yourself, in others, and in the world?

3. What do you, as a person, stand for?

4. What kind of impact do you want to make on the world? How do you want to contribute?

5. What kind of men do you respect?

6. What kind of men are you attracted to (qualities rather than physical attributes)?

7. What kind of men cause you to feel comfortable and relaxed?

8. What qualities in men turn you on or light you up?

9. List some of your favorite things. Think about things or experiences that he could give you: chocolates, white roses, the Sunday NY Times and a great cappuccino, star-gazing.

10. List some favorite hotspots. Keep it general, e.g., little hole in the wall ethnic restaurants, clubs with great music, cabins on the coast, rather than specific, e.g., Taj Indian Restaurant, Yoshi's, The Mendocino Inn and Cabins. Give him a sense of what you like, and then let him apply his creativity and resources.

11. List what you like to do for fun. Same as above – general, rather than specific: fun games, camping, kicking around bookstores, rather than parasailing, playing Apples & Oranges, backpacking to Lost Man's Creek, visiting Powell's in Portland.

12. Describe what it is about your work that causes you to feel happy or fulfilled. Describe the essence of your work.

30

Profile Template

Here is a template based on the answers to the previous questions which follows the structure that I described in Chapter 28. This is the actual text from a client's profile on Match. She consistently received messages from new men for three years using these words. I worked with her to craft the words, but all of the ideas are hers.

I am a curious, adventurous, romantic woman. I enjoy the surprises in life and the fact that every day brings different opportunities and experiences. I am often inspired with a fairly irreverent sense of humor. I am playful and I love to laugh, explore, dance, and express my individuality.

I value authenticity and openness. I thrive on beauty and the triumph of substance over flash. Being awake to the world and all of its possibilities in an atmosphere of integrity and joy is my footprint. I hope that my individuality is an asset to those that I impact.

I respect men who are intelligent, open-minded and articulate.

Confident, generous men who can take the lead with both authority and gentleness are attractive to me.

I feel comfortable and relaxed with men who are accepting, emotionally fluent, and who ask great questions and listen well to the answers. I like the feeling when a man has my back.

I think that a man who is romantic is sexy… The little details, holding hands, good conversation by firelight…

No drugs or heavy drinking, please.

Note: You may follow these guidelines and template and find that when your profile text is complete, it feels inadequate. You may have thoughts like, *"I didn't really say anything specific about myself,"* or *"This is so boring. If I was a guy, I'd pass on this one,"* or *"There's nothing of me in it."* These are common sentiments for women who have habitually interacted with NATs because NATs want you to engage and entertain them. They are *not* interested in you if it's clear that you value your own feelings and pleasure more than you will value them. A MM will like it when you speak about your feelings, your joy, and your inner experience. He is not looking to find out whether you will complement and care for him. He is looking to find out if you are happy, and open to be made happier. Trust me on this, and give it a shot. See what happens.

31

Pictures, Pictures, Pictures

I cannot stress too strongly the importance and impact of the right photos. Like it or not, I will say it again: most men are extremely visual. Your photos are the first line of presentation, and might be the last if they're not congruent with your feminine essence. This is where the, "*I just want a guy who loves me for me,*" and the "*What you see is what you get. Take it or leave it,*" school of thinking crumbles.

As I mentioned before, men are attracted to beauty and color, and presenting the most man-friendly version of your beauty will allow these guys to recognize and be drawn to you. Once in the visual door, they become interested in the "inner you." But the "outer you" needs to invite them through the gate. Just like a woman needs the soulful sensitivity, intelligence, and generosity of spirit in a man's words, he needs the beauty and receptivity in her visual presentation. When I work with women who have been disappointed with their previous online dating experiences, this is usually where the first and biggest tweaks occur. If you can, trust my guidance on this. I know it's kind of a pain in the aspiration to do several photo shoots until you get them right, but the payoff is palpable.

I have frequently heard men say that they will hold off on getting excited about a woman until they know that she actually looks like her photos. We want shots that are beautiful, current, and congruent with your essence and vibrancy.

If you're resentful about the fact that how you look matters so much, do what it takes to get over it. It's not bad. It doesn't mean that he's objectifying you. Men are attracted to women who wear color and emphasize their beauty in a certain manner. In particular, men are attracted to women who wear red. There are some fun scientific studies on the web about this, and it remains a fact.

Primary Photo
- High-resolution photos that capture your beauty, your joy, your spirit, your confidence, and your receptivity.
- A primary photo from the waist or bust up, where the lighting compliments your skin tone, with no shine. It is my experience that it's sometimes difficult to avoid shine, glare, or shadows with indoor photos unless a professional photographer takes them. Outdoor photos taken on an overcast day, with some beautiful, colorful nature behind you are very effective, and are often much easier for an amateur photographer, such as a friend, to capture. Hair that is soft and loose, and makeup that accentuates your beauty and personal style is a must. For this photo, wear a primarily single-colored top in reds, burgundies, corals, peach or blue with an attractive neckline, preferably with some skin showing in a manner that feels sensual but not trashy: neck, chest, possibly a little cleavage, arms. A lower neckline works best if you're wearing a necklace. We want a warm smile with receptive, joyful eyes looking at the camera.

Alternate photos
There are three other kinds of photos that are great if you can get them:
- An outdoorsy shot (hiking or biking clothes, sunglasses, hat), a "Let's play" look.
- A full body shot in a nice dress, in a setting that brings out your class and femininity.
- Any other photos that bring out your joy, sensuality, playfulness, and integrity.

- Avoid photos with other people, unless they are clearly family members. No girlfriend or pet shots, by and large, and definitely no photos with another man unless it's obviously Dad.

Caveat: if you have photos of yourself that you love, and they go against some of the advice I've given above, feel free to include them. You need to feel good about yourself in the images that you present. Just make sure that you have a primary photo that falls in line with what I've described above.

Remember that he is not looking at your photos to figure out if you're *interesting*. He's looking at your photos to ascertain whether you are *happy, beautiful, and energetically available.*

32

Anonymity

When you are anonymous online, you assume a position of femininity and safety: feminine because you are waiting for him to earn the right to know you, and even to know your name, and safe because you can wait until you have a good sense of a man before disclosing your identity. I encourage women to remain anonymous until they're preparing for a first phone call or first in-person meeting.

In service to these principles, I suggest that you create an anonymous email address that corresponds with your username. That way, if, for some reason, he wants to move the communication onto his private email, you can communicate and still remain anonymous. When you sign up for a normal email address, say on gmail, you give your actual first and last names as part of the sign up information. Then, when someone receives an email from you in their inbox, it lists your actual name as the sender. We want an email address that will list an anonymous name as the sender.

So, here is how to create an anonymous email address. Go to gmail and sign up for a new account that corresponds with your username (e.g., if your username is CrystalRose you'll make some version of the email address, say crystalrose8888@gmail.com. In the sign up information, rather than using your true first and last names, use the first part of your username (Crystal) for your first name, and the second part of your username (Rose) as your last name. If your username has only one word in it, make up a pretty last name. Then, when you correspond with him privately, your identity will still be protected. Use this address as your sign up email address for whatever online dating sites you choose.

33

Where to Post

I suggest that you open two sites simultaneously to start this dating adventure. A good "pay to date" site with high volume, like match.com or yahoosingles, is a great basecamp. You're likely to get a lot of traffic, and these are reputable sites with many people who are looking for a relationship. Also, larger sites often have optional real time components, like local singles events, or work with an in-house matchmaker, which might be nice perks further down the road.

Next, open a second site that might be a little more matched to your particular interests or lifestyle – Spiritual Singles, Christian Singles, Green Singles, etc. If you google online dating sites including a keyword – cycling, fitness, your profession, ivy league college, social activism, etc. – you'll find lots of choices.

As an alternative, you might want to choose a high-volume free site like Plentyoffish. It will give you a little more diverse crowd to sort through, but you'll find some diamonds.

If you've habitually chosen NATs in the past, or if you're prone to over-giving, I suggest you wait to register with sites that go deeper into personal matching criteria. Some sites invite more intimate discussions or disclosures as an initial way to get to know prospective suitors – sites like EHarmony or Chemistry. The invitation to dive too deep, too fast, and then start to take care of his feelings can be challenging. They're great sites, but wait until your feminine is well-anchored before engaging with them.

See the following section on Apps for a few other perspectives regarding sites.

34

Dating Apps

It's a new world of dating with a preponderance of dating apps. And there are lots of different kinds of apps, from reputable online sites like Zoosk, Match, and OKCupid, to hook up apps like Pure and Down. Although there are many pros to being able to do your dating from your phone, I want *first* to speak to a few possible cons.

A lot of the appeal of apps is convenience. Coffee Meets Bagel's byline is "designed for singles who want to find something real with little or no effort." Often convenience is the enemy of courtship. The feeling of being courted lives in the realm of being pursued and cherished. As I've already mentioned, healthy, generous, cherishing men tend to fall in love when they give, and healthy, feminine women tend to fall in love when they receive. In the dance of courtship men need chasing space and women need breathing space. Men need to put themselves on the line and risk, and women need to stay in touch with their feelings, their bodies, and their connection to pleasure. When things are too easy for men, they can become complacent and self-centered, and lose the ability to fall in love. When women take too much initiative, give too much, and are too available, they can become brittle and objectifying, and *their* ability to fall in love is hindered. In fact, when women do too much, unless they are extremely anchored in high self-esteem and femininity, they will begin to believe that courtship and being cherished by a man is a fairy tale, at which point they focus on chemistry and compatibility (is he hot and do we like the same things) and engage in relationships which will usually plateau into friends with benefits pretty quickly.

It is probably busy, high performance people who are most enchanted with apps. Convenience and expedience are the watchwords.

With some apps, like Tinder, the criteria is, initially, visually based. If you like the way he looks swipe right, and if not, left. A problem here is that, as we've talked about before, healthy MMs are not vain, so their pics often aren't great. If you're a woman, and you don't know how to decipher those pics, chances are you'll swipe away men who will never have the option of contacting you since both parties have to "swipe" each other before a message can be sent. Also, for men, this app reduces risk. They don't have to suck it up and take the risk of reaching out to a woman who may or may not be interested in him, and those risks require some testosterone. When a man knows that a woman is interested in him, he can relax a bit when he approaches her, and for generous, cherishing men, that relaxation isn't always a good thing. These guys become more enlivened, creative, and interested in what or who they are pursuing when they have to jump over some obstacles to get there. Conversely, busy women, in the middle of a busy day, go to their phone and can quickly sort through or respond to men without ever having to switch out of their "get it on and get it done" energy, and that's not a good place to be when courtship is in question.

So, when things are made easier for men, and things go faster for women, not so good. Also, the whole paradigm of cell phones often has a lot to do with immediacy. Texting can almost demand instant access to the person being texted, and it's very important for women to give men some chasing space. Plus, some apps are designed for immediate response. Couple that with a site like Bumble where women do the initiating, and you've got a recipe for short-term gratification resulting in a role reversal that is extremely difficult to turn around later. When women put it in motion, the romantic dance will often result in men who don't initiate, which is one of the biggest complaints that I hear from women. (Caveat: If you are looking for a man who is 63 or older, you can do more initiating. So Bumble might be a viable option for you.)

There are some nice pros to using dating apps. A lot of people are using them, so there's a wide pool of people – probably people you wouldn't necessarily find on online dating sites. There can be a freshness and fun to expanding the dating world through your phone. And the sites are pretty specific in their focus and tools, so that can really narrow down the random factors in meeting people.

If you are inclined to participate in dating apps, and you want to keep the dance of courtship strongly engaged, here are some suggestions:

- Do some research. Get a google search going and learn about the various apps on the menu.
- If you just want to hook up or get laid, go for the ones especially designed for that, like Pure and Down.
- If you are interested in courtship, I suggest that before you respond to any message on an app, you relax and get in touch with your body. Don't quickly steal away from your work for a few minutes and make checking your apps one more thing on your To Do list.
- If you're going to use a site that is appearance based, like Tinder, get to know how masculine men present themselves in their pics.
- Breathe – a lot. Move slowly. If he messages you, give it a day before you get back to him. Do not feel the need to respond quickly or in kind. You'll need to shed any of those great "I know exactly how to put other people at ease" tendencies and let him be the guy, reach out to you, make the plan, and wait for you to get back to him.
- Once you have responded, let him know as soon as possible that you'd prefer to be contacted by a call or email, not texting. Get off the app expediently.

I think you can have some fun and meet some great guys using dating apps. Just keep your feminine front and center.

35

Reading and Responding to Emails

Let the games begin!

The purpose of this phase of communication is to begin to recognize the three major players in the world of cyber suitors – MMs, NATs, and MATs. Once you can recognize them, you will continue to fortify your own feminine perceptions, energetics, and behavior in relation to these men so you can allow healthy courtship to evolve.

The initial skills you will exercise focus on learning to discern who's who by the way they communicate with you, and by reading how and what they present in their profiles. As you become more adept at this discernment, you will appropriately release the men who do not treat you well. Then you can move on to the business of encouraging the men you want to get to know, learning how to allow them to pursue and cherish you as you move into phone and, eventually, in-person contact.

36

How to Spot Them – Decrypting First Emails

Okay so you're set. Your profile is crafted and your pictures rock. It's time to run it up the flagpole, so to speak, and see who salutes.

If you've done online dating before, in all probability your habit is to go to your inbox, check out the list of messages, and then you do either one of two things:

1. You briefly scan the message and go right to the sender's profile to see his pictures. If he's attractive enough to proceed, you take a look at what he says about himself to determine whether your interests and philosophies mesh. If he passes those two tests, maybe you send him a quick note right away and move on to the next guy.

Or:

2. You don't even read his message. You go directly to his profile, and then proceed with everything outlined in choice #1.

Am I right?

If so, you're demonstrating that your criteria for even giving the guy the time of day is based on chemistry and compatibility.

The problem with this approach is that you miss the most critical factor in getting your dating process started on the right foot, and that factor is **how does he treat you?**

All three types of cyber suitors will pretty much announce who they are and how you can expect to be treated by them right up front.

So when I work with clients, we look closely at what announcements are contained in that first email before looking at his profile. Once we've ascertained who is probably who, we go to the profile to cross check that information. Understanding how to decrypt, first of all, the initial emails, and then the profiles, suddenly puts you in the position of making informed decisions in a whole new way.

Here's how...

37

First Emails

Let's take a look at how MMs will generally approach a woman online.

Remember that these men will look at your profile like a job description. The job they're trying to land is getting a shot at increasing the happiness, comfort, safety, and relaxation of a pleasure-fluent woman: you. They will examine your pictures to see if your joy, confidence, and spark are apparent, and then they will read what you say about yourself to see if that backs up their initial impression. If it does, they will read on to see what kind of men you like. If the profile is written in language that speaks to them, they will study it and assess whether or not they think they can fit the bill. Having gone that far, they will contact you. If they email you, this next section will help you recognize them.

They will almost always do one or more of the following things in a first email:

1. There will be a subject line that is somewhere between friendly and effusive: *"Hello!"* or *"Hello Beautiful,"* or *"Good Morning!"* or *"I noticed you love animals. Me, too!"*

Remember that MMs often can't think and feel at the same time, so they may be very enthusiastic, and sometimes use strange grammar or misspelled words. In the old days, you would have interpreted that to mean that you're dealing with a guy who is uneducated. Today, at first blush, we will assume that he's probably excited about you, and isn't accessing that left brain hemisphere much. Hold off on the judgment until we get to his profile. Oddly enough, guys who misspell

words are often very well-educated, and just dyed-in-the-wool masculine: not always, but often.

2. They will greet you in the body of the email, often with your
username:
"Hello Angelbaby," "Bonjour Belle Femme," etc.

3. They will give you a direct compliment: *"You are gorgeous!"*

4. They will try and entertain you in any number of ways: tell you
a joke, relay a funny story from their life, be witty or self-deprecating, or send you a link to something humorous.
"I've included a picture of me teaching my dog how to play poker."

5. They will "resumé" for you. By this, I mean that they will study
what you said that you were looking for in a man, and then
proceed to tell you how they are the guy for the job. When they
resumé, they will generally refer directly to the qualifications
you listed, and then explain their experience and expertise with
those qualifications. A lot of times women think that men are
bragging because they're egotistical. In fact, if you look closely,
you'll see that they read your profile closely and they're *lobbying*.
It's pretty endearing, once you see what's happening.
*"I love Lake Tahoe, too. In fact, I have a little cabin up there with
a big stone fireplace. It opens right up to the Nordic trails. I think
you'd really like it!"*

6. They will be directive in some way. Generally, their first directive is somewhere in the vicinity of, *"Please take a look at my
profile and let me know if you're interested."* But they might also
jump ahead a little and say something like, *"I'd love to take you
out for a drink or lunch."* (We like directive. It means that he's

willing to put it on the line and take the lead, so you're not left wondering what to do after some amorphous message with an inferred course of action but no real invitation, which we'll see later when we look at the other types of cyber-suitors.)

7. They will sign off in some way, and tell you their name:
"Cheers! Jack"
"Don't let the heat get to you, Chuck"
"Enjoy the weekend! Steve"

Like that.

Check out this example of an email from a masculine man to see what I'm talking about:
"Hi Angelina, (Greeting)
I couldn't help writing once I saw your beautiful smile and read your thoughtful text. (Direct compliments) *Hey, you said you like dogs. Have you seen the youtube video of the Golden rocking out to Santana? Here's the link. I think you'll get a good laugh.* (Entertaining her)
Anyway, I think I can pretty much say that I'm the guy that you were describing. I've got a good job where I make a difference in the quality of life in some third world countries. Plus I'm an avid camper and I'm always kind to kids and waiters. (Resumé) *Take a look at my profile and see if you're interested. I hope so!!!* (Directive)
Stay warm (Sign-off)
Bobby"

Classic.

38

What Comes Next – More Decryption

Next we go to the profile to see if it backs up what you've decrypted from his note. And, just like your profile is a congruent announcement that you are a woman available for cherishing, his profile will be a congruent announcement that he is a generous, cherishing man who is optimistic, successful, happy, and available. That's what we're looking for.

The next two chapters will cover his pictures and his text, and how to decipher the clues that identify his masculinity.

39

His Pictures

My friend, Katherine, likes to say, *"Well, if I was a student of the obvious..."* Being a student of the obvious means that I take what is presented at face value. Exercising this skill when it comes to looking at a man's online pictures is a great perspective, and it can also be interesting and amusing. Generally, MMs are not vain, and their self-esteem is pretty healthy, so their pics aren't great. They're more interested in showing you what they can do for you or give to you, rather than looking for pics that make them look really handsome. He already thinks that he looks pretty good most of the time, and if he's smiling, and his face looks open and happy, and you can see his eyes, in his assessment, that's good enough. He might be smiling, open-faced, lookin' right atcha, holding a big ol' bass that he caught in front of his naked torso, or he might be smiling, open-faced, lookin' right atcha, sitting on his Harley, or in the front seat of his cherry red vintage Camaro, or on his deck overlooking the Pacific Coast in his swim trunks, or sitting at an Italian outdoor café with an espresso. He wants you to see that he's a friendly, good guy, and then get right down to the business of showing you what he can give you.

Sometimes these guys will have one, dimly lit, full-body smiler, or a smiler selfie, and then they'll have, like, fifty pictures of pretty places in nature or birds or sunsets. All of this, in the great school of being a student of the obvious, translates to: *"I'm not that concerned with me. I want you to see that I'm a happy and safe person, but look over here at these nice places I can take you, or these pretty pictures of things that girls like. Are you happy, yet?"*

It's super-sweet.

And the good and sometimes confusing news is that, because they're not vain, and they often tend to make a poor showing with their pics online, when you meet them, they're often much more attractive than their pictures.

Really.

You'll want to say to them, *"What were you thinking? You're hot. Post some new photos. I'll take them. You look really good!"* So, the most interesting part of that response would be his answer to "What were you thinking?" Cause he wasn't thinking. He was excited about meeting some really beautiful women, and he wanted to get through the messy and unnatural tasks of trying to talk about himself and represent himself in a cyber medium as quickly as possible. That's also why the spelling and grammar in his profile may sometimes look crazy. He's not that interested in himself and he wants to get this thing done as quickly as possible. What he *is* interested in is getting a shot at being interested in *you*.

"I don't like to talk about myself. It sounds like I'm bragging."
First line from "Jack's" profile.

And that's pay dirt.

40

What He Says and How He Says It: Profile Text

Let's divide the information in his profile into seven sections:
1. Username and byline
2. Initial statistics (age, marital status, age range of women he's looking for, distance he's willing to travel, etc.)
3. The body of his text that talks about himself
4. Who he's looking for
5. His interests and lifestyle information
6. His occupation and income
7. Anything else, such as faith and education

1. Usernames and Bylines

We're back to being a student of the obvious with this one. As a governing principle, MMs aren't crazy about this medium of meeting women, but they understand the practicality of diving into this big pool of available women. Since they don't particularly like to talk about why they're so great, they will rush through the process of getting a profile up, and hope it's enough to warrant a date.

Consequently, things like usernames and bylines are utilitarian. They will often have usernames that *look* utilitarian: Jim1996, or 97520SF, or JLSF_1950: initials, zip codes, birth years all seem good enough. Or they will take a stab at some descriptive adjectives or action-oriented nouns: Wildmanjack, Runnerdude, CrazybutFun: nothing too sexy, and usually it will be innocuous or clueless.

With their bylines it's a little different. Often they will use a short phrase that already gets into what he can do for you: *"Let's explore the world!" "Dancing, dining, travel," "Life is better when you share it with someone special.*" Generally, they will not preach, teach, or control, as NATs might, with by-lines like: *"Let your hair down," "Silence is golden," "Drama queens need not apply."*

Throughout their entire profiles, a litmus test about whether you're dealing with a MM is how you *feel* when you read what he has written. If you feel relaxed, neutral, and safe, with no big adrenalin charge, no fear mixed with excitement, and no self-doubt, you're on the right track. You will feel neutral or comfortable in the presence of MMs, both on the page and in person. This is one of the reasons why you want to be relaxed, comfortable, and unhurried when you read a suitor's online profile. You want to be paying close attention to *how you feel*, which is sometimes a subtle art, so you need to be gently and presently inhabiting your body. (We'll get into this subject in depth in the upcoming *"Feminine Rituals" chapter.*)

2. Initial Statistics

One of the few things that MMs may fudge on a little is their height, whereas women tend to fudge on weight and age. So be prepared. With their relationship stats, what you want to see is that he's divorced, widowed, or never married. "Currently Separated" seems to be a category that a lot of women allow if there's chemistry happening. But my experience, played out repeatedly, is that "Currently Separated" means "Still Married." Even when a man has been living apart from his wife for a long time, or she's already seeing someone else, or he says that the romance is gone and they've been living like roommates for a while now – all of that means "Still Married." And when people get divorced, they often change in ways that they cannot anticipate once the divorce is finalized. When those changes occur, the woman who has agreed to date him before he's divorced usually gets the short end of the stick. That short end looks like this man suddenly realizing that he actually needs some time to be single, or that, for some inexplicable reason, he's losing his attraction to the new woman. He's apologetic, and he may make some kind of declarations or oaths that he'll be back after he has some space to work out a few things, blah, blah, blah. Usually those men *don't* return to the new woman, and sometimes it can even transpire in a manner that makes her feel sorry for him as he's leaving. It's super-gnarly, and I suggest that you don't go there to begin with. If a man who is "Currently Separated" contacts you, it's fine to let him know that he seems like a great guy and you'd be happy to hear from him once his divorce has been finalized for six months.

Case closed.

MMs will often have a large age range for the women they're interested in meeting. It's common that they'll have a 15 to 20-year span in there, like "40–60" or "32–51." And as far as the radius in which they're looking, that will also often be fairly substantial: "within 100 miles of Manhattan Beach." Younger guys may have a little narrower age range (women 36–47), and a little wider geographic radius (within 300 miles of Manhattan Beach), and with men over 57ish it may be the opposite: broader age range (women 42–67) and narrower geographic radius (within 50 miles of Manhattan Beach). All of this contrasts with more narcissistic men who will be narrow in both categories (women 32–40, within 15 miles of Manhattan Beach) because they want what they want in terms of the age of their future hostage, and they don't want to have to travel far to get it.

3. When He Writes About Himself

Bottom line: a MM is fairly clueless about *what* to say about himself. His best guess is that you'll want to know that he's healthy, has a good job, and is financially sound, and also that he's a good guy who can show you a good time. He'll often want you to know about what and who he values, and he'll like sharing with you some of the prominent aspects of his lifestyle so that you can realistically assess whether or not you might be compatible. He probably won't feel entirely comfortable touting his assets, so you can expect to see one of two things when he is telling you what's good about himself:

He'll use a phrase like, *"My friends tell me that I'm...* (easy on the eyes, really dependable, fun to be around, funny, etc.).

He'll speak positively about his looks or his character, and then he'll be slightly self-deprecating: *"I'm athletic and in good shape (for my age),"* or *"I have a good sense of humor (at least my dog thinks so)."*

Remember that, in general, these guys tend toward brevity, so you can bet you're dealing with a MM if his profile text is short and to the point, especially if it meets the above qualifications. Look for exclamation points, caps, and weird spelling or grammatical mistakes since they're ripping this thing off as quickly as possible.

4. When They Talk About You

MMs need women who are warm, flexible, good-natured, and happy. They value women who take good care of themselves, who enjoy life, who don't sweat the small stuff, and who are made of strong moral fiber. They definitely need women who will respect men, and have room in their lives for a relationship. They want to know that you are fairly autonomous and can take care of yourself financially, even though they'll want to provide for you. They find self-assured, authentic, receptive, and responsive women very attractive.

That's about it.

Really.

Unlike more narcissistic men, a MM is not looking for a woman who will focus on making *him* happy, seek to entertain *him*, or make sure *his* pleasure is handled before her own. On the other hand, a narcissistic man will have a lot to say about what *he* wants.

Sometimes MMs will say very little about what kind of woman they are seeking. This is because they're thoughtful, and don't want you to feel pressured by their preferences. They might just say something like, "*What am I looking for? Well, what are we all looking for? A wonderful woman I can share my life with,*" and then they'll just finish up and get out of there. More often, they will talk a little about who and what they want in terms that are fairly gentle.

"*I'd like to meet a woman who knows herself and will probably laugh at my jokes. It would be nice if she likes to be out in nature fairly often. If she enjoys travel and fine dining, that's a plus.*"

5. Interests and Lifestyle Information

Optimism, energy, playfulness, generosity - all of these terms apply to MMs. So, generally, they enjoy and engage with life. This shows up in their interests and the choices they make about the structure of their lives. Typically, they will enjoy some sports, physical fitness activities, travel, and hobbies. They will frequently be life-long learners, and talk a little about being stimulated by new places and people, or adventure, or leisure activities that involve some kind of fun self-expansion. They may talk about future visions, and will want you to have a part in those. They generally value their friends and family, and put parenting at a high premium if that's part of their world. They are not shy to speak about challenges, but will do so in terms that emphasize lessons learned or value gained. And because they are built to thrive when they give, often they will speak about *how* they give: volunteering, mentoring, something about the focus of their work, spending time with their kids or grandkids.

6. His Occupation and Income

These men have usually defined themselves in a strong manner through their work, and they are proud of, and fulfilled by, what they do, or have done. Pay close attention to how they speak about their work, if they are still working. It's also not unusual for a man who is retired to talk a bit about the fulfilling career that he enjoyed before retirement. They are also not shy to speak about their financial situation. They want you to have a clear picture of where they stand and what you can expect in terms of their ability to provide, and the kind of lifestyle you can anticipate if you get involved with him. Often they will have no preference about your income, or if they do, it will probably look something like needing for you to let them know that you make enough to stand on your own two feet. These guys don't want to be objectified for their net worth, so they need to know that you can rely on yourself financially, when necessary. But beyond that, they are generous and providing.

7. Anything Else

MMs are honest men. They are also discrete so they won't over-disclose, especially if they feel like they might be taken for granted or used. But they generally don't lead with those defenses, because they veer toward optimism and feeling that people are basically good. Consequently, you can expect for them to be honest about who they are, what they believe, and their education, spiritual life, and background. They like themselves, and what you see is usually what you can expect to get.

41

The Contrast: How NATs Show Up Online

Narcissism is a complex personality disorder. Once more, I want to be clear that when I speak about this category of men, I am not necessarily speaking about those with this disorder. I am not a therapist, and such disorders are not my area of expertise. I am speaking about men with some narcissistic tendencies. As stated earlier, these guys are interested in finding out whether or not you will increase *their* pleasure, comfort, and well-being, whether or not you will take the lead and do the heavy lifting, and whether or not you are a candidate for protecting, providing for, and cherishing *them*. No doubt you will encounter men with the bona fide diagnosis, but we want to weed out the darker shades of gray in this category, which will allow you to swerve around anyone who announces, early on, that they fall anywhere near these tendencies.

When women have been groomed by narcissistic parents or partners in the past, one of the features of that grooming is a certain aversion to boundaries and clear assessment skills. Narcissistic people want to throw their victims off balance, and keep them off balance for the purpose of retaining power in the relationship. Consequently, they teach their victims to question their own reality, to be unsure and insecure, and to always look to themselves as the problem if something doesn't feel good in the relationship.

Ouch.

When it comes to assessing what kind of men you might be dealing with, based on how they present themselves in their emails and profiles, I often find that women with those histories resist my decryption process. They frequently say things like, *"Well, how do you know that it's always true (about whatever features I may be discussing)?"* or *"Everybody deserves a chance. People can change."* or *"It just seems so judgmental to look at a man that way. You put people in boxes."* Meanwhile, these same women will usually be very attracted to NATs and end up with the same old progressively depleting and discouraging endgame.

One of the most effective ways to know that you're dealing with a man who will not be good for you is how you feel when you look at his pics and read what he's written. If you feel anything other than confident, comfortable in your own skin, and relaxed, you're probably looking at a NAT. But I will outline some information that will help you back that up.

Decrypting First Emails

Emotionally seductive, assumptive, vague, controlling, stingy, complacent, driven, confusing – all of these adjectives apply. NATs will read your vulnerabilities and play on them hard.

Unlike MMs, NATs may or may not put in a subject line. Often they don't greet you, or if they do, it is casual or over the top.

"Hey..." (casual)

"Hello Goddess!!!" (over the top)

In the body of the email they can swing from feeding you crumbs to, again, being way too much.

"I'm going to be in San Francisco the end of April. I could use a tour guide." (crumbs)

"Clearly the angels broke the mold after they created you. I would love to take such an intriguing woman to a romantic dinner next Saturday. Would you do me the honor?" (way too much)

Sometimes they make disparaging comments about other women they have seen on line, and then cap it by telling you why you're so much better than those women.

"I was just about to get off of this site because I couldn't handle reading

about one more woman who loves "walks on the beach." Then I came across your intelligence and style. What a relief!"

If they're directive, usually they will make an offer, sort of, without reference to your comfort.

"We should have drinks."

"We're almost neighbors. Maybe we should get together."

Often they'll say things that infer no course of action, which may or may not reference something in your profile, and you're left wondering how to respond.

"Raiders season is about to start."

"The driftwood on the coast is outrageous this year."

Maybe they sign off, maybe they don't. All in all you probably feel confused, a little off balance, and/or revved up.

Let's take a look at how NATs may "out" themselves in their profiles.

A. Their Pictures

These are the guys that you're probably habitually attracted to, because they look *good*. These are vain men who post pics where they look hot. They are usually insecure guys who need a lot of reinforcement, and looking great in their online pics is one way they do it. Continuing in the "student of the obvious" line of assessment, they will often give other clues about themselves in their pics, clues that say, in a sense, *"It's all about me, and whether or not you please me."*

Here are some of those clues: he's not smiling in most of his pics (except the one with his dog), he's wearing sun glasses, he has another disembodied arm or hand around his shoulder from another woman who has been cut out of the picture, he will be sitting back in a kind of balls-out, "show me whatcha got" kind of posture, he will be dressed in black, he will be walking away, or his body will be guarded in some manner. That's a start.

B. Their Words

1. Username and Bylines

Unlike MMs who create extremely utilitarian names like JRK1950 or SF0007, NATs will want to let you know what they like (so you can already be considering how to provide it for them) or how cool they are, or they will announce that you will have to *earn* admission to their inner sanctums. So their usernames will often either announce what *their* interests are: "Runningcyclingskiing," "Marathonman," or what's so great about them: "Kindgenerousbrave," "Worldtraveler22," or a strange name that obviously means something, but you don't get to know, *just yet*: "Enigman2882," or "Quantumidean." None of these usernames say anything about you and what he can do for you, but, in fact, start to groom you to think about how cool he is, and what *you* might have to do to make *him* like *you*.

Ick.

As far as bylines go, again you can expect to either be told how cool he is (*"Great guy who knows how to love"*), what he likes and wants (*"Seeking a woman who makes my heart beat faster"*), schooling (*"It's not about half full or half empty, but how you perceive the glass"*), or something off the wall that will throw you a little off balance (*"slam dance, heartcrush, love at first sight"*). You can pretty much bet that whatever he says he is, he isn't. It's a strange emotional vortex that these guys set up where they announce who and what they are in glowing terms, so that when they turn out to *not* be that, it's quite confusing. At that point it can definitely make you question *your* reality because you're immersed in *their* reality. Count on it being crazy-making.

2. Initial Statistics

Remember that these men don't want to exert themselves, and they want to keep most of their cards hidden. Some obvious ways that this shows up is tight age ranges for the women that they're seeking (women 32–41), a tighter geographic radius where they're willing to look, (within 15 miles of San Francisco), and the exclusion of certain data up front, like how much he drinks, how much he earns, or marital status.

3. When He Writes About Himself

A lot: that's often the first clue in this section. He goes on and on. It's not unusual for MMs to write a paragraph or two, as outlined before. But NATs like to talk about themselves, and they do it easily. They have no problem telling you what's so great about them, (*"I'm considerate, handsome, intellectual, well-read, intuitive, etc, etc, etc."*), and they have no problem telling you what they like, which may or may not have anything to do with what he can, or will, provide for you (*"I'm an avid skier who participated in the Winter Games in 2002, I enjoy great times with great friends, weekends I cycle up Mt. Bachelor with my cycling club, the Bahamas are my second home, etc., etc., etc."*). They also are prone to a slightly self-righteous moral stance, expressed with some "tude." Here's an example: *"I believe that the world is just waiting to wake up, and that humans play their parts in this global drama by exercising increased compassion, forgiveness, and tolerance"* (which is a preview of some of the qualities he will demand from you). NATs will often talk about kissing and cuddling, and even love-making in their profiles. They will start immediately schooling you about the sensual activities that make them feel good. Might sound nice, but beware.

4. When They Talk About You

These dudes will generally have no problem listing their extensive criteria for the women they might possibly consider getting to know, often "as friends first." (FYI, when men talk about being "friends first" in a profile, it's generally an announcement that they're not going to pay for the date.) They may use the word "should" when speaking about their criteria for the women they want (*"She should be intellectually awake and aware while retaining her feminine mystique*"). They will usually outline a micro-managed version of who they want you to be, and it will often be a lot about what you can do for him, or how you compliment him: in other words, it will be "him" referenced:

> *"I'm looking for a woman who shares my passion for travel."*
> *"I'm looking for a woman who makes my heart beat faster every time she walks in the room."*
> *"I'm looking for a woman who is loyal, honest, a giver."*
> *"I'm looking for a woman who is a one-man woman."*

Then they may tell you what you can't be:

> *"No drama queens."*
> *"No divas."*
> *"No heavy baggage."*
> *"No gold diggers need apply."*
> *"If you don't have a picture, don't bother emailing."*

5. Interests and Lifestyle Information

Again, these men want for you to know what pleases them, so that you can provide for them. They will probably list a lot of very specific activities or travel destinations, or lifestyle preferences. They think they're cool, and they want you to think that they're cool so that they can begin the process of fostering your adoration, dependence, and obsession.

6. Income and Occupation

In the movie, *Julie and Julia*, Julia Child is in her bridge class in Paris, and the bridge teacher says, "*Ladies, breast your cards.*" In other words, hold them close to you so no one can see what you've got. NATs breast their cards in the arena of their money. Often they will not list their income, but have criteria for what yours needs to be.

If they do list theirs, you can count on them wanting yours to be as much, if not more. They want reciprocity, at the very least, and always. These are the guys who are keeping score of what they give, and it always comes with a price. These are the kind of men who taught you not to let a guy pay for dinner, because if you do, you owe him.

They generally do not have a problem listing their occupations, unless what they list might insinuate that they have a lot of money, in which case, they will tell you later.

So if he looks good in his pics and he tells you what a great guy he is so that when you start feeling bad with him you know, for sure, that *you're* the problem, you're probably looking at a NAT. If he tells you that you might have the good luck of being one of the women who could possibly interest him if you can meet all of his criteria, you're probably looking at a NAT. If he lets you know what he likes and how he likes it done so you can get busy trying to marshal all of your inner and outer resources to try and win him, it's NAT time.

42

The Three Internal Signs That You're Dealing with a NAT

There is a fairly foolproof test for assessing whether or not you're dealing with a NAT. The test has to do with how you feel as you are interacting with him online, on the phone, or on date. If you experience one of the following internal signals during or after dealing with him, it's a big yellow flag. If you experience two or three, it's time to retreat and reassess.

1. Your self-esteem tanks. You know how that feels – low-energy, shame, depression, negative self-talk.

2. You feel confused. You don't know what to do in response to him, or you don't understand what's happening in regard to him.

3. You begin to second-guess yourself. You may have thoughts like, *"Did I read that right?"* or *"Maybe I came on too strong and I scared him,"* or *"Maybe I wasn't effusive enough."* You're looking for clues in your past behavior, communications, or perceptions that might explain why you don't feel good now, or why he seems to have changed, or has gone MIA, etc.

It's good to share these with your dating buddy so she can help you recognize what's going on. Often, if you're in deep enough to experience these, it can be difficult to see and/or admit the signs. You may have some substantial oxytocin happening, which will cause you to minimize what doesn't work and maximize the options for staying bonded to him. Make sure you stay current with another neutral dating friend regularly.

43

How MATs Present Themselves

This is an enjoyable little piece of sleuthing. As I mentioned before, what we're dealing with here is a man who is essentially masculine, and has had women do too much for him, so he's become somewhat complacent. Consequently, his profile will give you some mixed messages. As with all profiles, you're going to make a best guess based on the sum total of indicators.

A MAT will probably set up those mixed messages in his first communication to you. Perhaps he doesn't greet you, and he's a little assumptive about getting together, but he uses a ton of exclamation points, and he lays a big, beautiful direct compliment on you.

> *"I see that we both live in Fairfield. That always makes it easier!!*
> *We should get together sometime and have a drink, since you're so*
> *outrageously beautiful!!!*
> *Ciao,*
> *Jason"*

If you feel a little confused, or you're not quite sure what to do in response to his note, but you feel relaxed and confident as you read it, then that's the first indication that this may be a MAT.

You proceed to his profile. His primary picture looks kind of hot, but then there are three or four goofy selfies that make you laugh.

His user name is innocuous, but his byline is a little arrogant.

> *Jason2344 "What's up?"*

When he talks about himself, maybe he writes a lot, but in the midst of it he's self-deprecating, or shows some piece of his heart. Maybe he talks about wanting a woman who "should be" blah blah

blah, but then he finishes off his writing with something generous and a little humble.

> *"Thanks for taking the time to read my profile, beautiful! Hope to hear from you!"*

Like that.

If you are wondering whether this guy is a MAT, the litmus test is how you feel after surveying the scene: if you still feel comfortable and relaxed, and he seems benign, and maybe a little clueless, probably a MAT.

What that means is that it's your job to go *super-fem* on him. Take at least 48 hours to respond, give him the clear indication of how good what he offered made you feel, and simply respond to his requests. Don't get chatty, don't answer inferred questions, keep it short, sweet, and receptive.

> *"Hi Jason,*
> *I enjoyed your sweet email.*
> *I like your idea of getting together for a drink. What did you have in mind?*
> *Lily"*

MATs are generally men who are very attractive, powerful, and/or wealthy, and they are discouraged by women who try too hard to please them. When they encounter a woman who keeps herself securely in her feminine when interacting with him, and makes him work to win her, they blossom. It's a wonderful thing to behold.

So if you think you've been contacted by a MAT, practice the same skills that you would exercise with a MM, and watch the magic happen.

44

Oxytocin

Oxytocin.

Ahhhh… The love potion…

It is a chemical cascade that supports you in procreation and it wants you to *bond*. So it will conjure up feel-good associations with the object of its intended bonding, in this case a man. It will allow you to forget what doesn't work with your guy, and amplify what does. It may catalyze protective instincts (as in you protecting him), or mothering instincts (equally sticky). It's strong, and it takes a while to detox from it. It's not bad. We just don't want to encourage its production until you've had enough clear-headed interactions with a man to know that he's a good prospect with whom to bond. It is released when women orgasm, *but it usually released in men only when they orgasm with someone that they love.*

It often stays in the bloodstream for a long time, thus the importance of going slowly and allowing plenty of time between dates.

Here is a partial list of feelings and behaviors that can occur from an oxytocin hit.

Increased bonding
Increased feelings of trust and reduction of fear
Increased generosity
Sexual arousal
Maternal behavior
Inhibition of certain memory functions
Defensive aggression against outsiders

So, take it easy. No sex, or even hand-holding or kissing for a while. Understand that the internal chemicals are strong, and respect them. It's good to have those chemicals swirling around inside of us when there's a good man and a good reason, but don't lose your head on the approach. Move slowly so the oxytocin can build once it's safe to step into a relationship, and you've got a MM or a developing MAT to step alongside.

Don't waste your love potion on a NAT.

*Oxytocin is released in many different kinds of relationships, e.g., parent/child, galpals. We are focusing here on its ability to impact romantic relationships.

45

Back to the Process: Responding to Initial Emails

He's sent you an initial email. You've checked out his profile. He seems masculine. What comes next?

After reminding yourself that even though his pics aren't great (or even good), he looks happy, he's smiling at the camera, and he will probably look a lot more attractive in person. Set aside the old compatibility criteria for the time being in deference to the fact that he's treating you well, and your body feels comfortable and relaxed when you look at his message and profile, and go ahead and respond. (Be aware that you're probably making this decision based on my criteria, not based on any real sense of excitement or interest. That's okay – just follow instructions for now.) So *how* do you respond, and when?

Let's address the when first: if he's 57 or younger, his testosterone levels are probably still high, so I suggest that you wait for 24–72 hours before writing back.

Game-playing?

Nope.

Principle: MMs need chasing space. They become vitalized when they have to work for, and wait for, what they want (unlike NATs who want for you to make everything easy and immediate). MMs also fall in love when they give, and deferring to your timing is one form of giving (unlike NATs who never fall in love with anyone but themselves). They will like women who are relaxed and confident, women who reference their own sense of comfort before his. (Remember that you're learning who these men really are, and you're interacting with them according to that new learning.)

So, if the man is 57 or younger, this is why I suggest that you wait for 72 hours to respond.

If your guy is 58–65, you need to try and get a read on his testosterone level. Is he eager and enthusiastic about you? Does he use exclamation points? Does he seem energized? Does he give you direct compliments and present a definite plan? If these are present you're probably dealing with a guy who still needs some substantial chasing space. Give it 24–48 hours before responding. (Because he's in the hormone crossover zone, 72 hours might be a little long.)

For men 66 and older, I'd wait for 24 hours unless he's clearly presenting with a lot of need for "chase." Men whose testosterone levels are lower will connect in a slightly more feminine manner, using vernacular like, *"I love so and so,"* or *"I enjoy blah blah blah,"* and they may be slightly less directive, e.g., *"It would be nice to get to know you,"* or *"It seems like we have a lot in common. I'd be interested in seeing where this could go."* Their compliments may be more indirect, e.g., *"I could feel the joy in your pictures,"* or *"I loved it when you talked about emotional honesty in your profile."* You will probably find that these men are very chivalrous when they meet you in person. They will just be a little softer around the edges, a little more immediately in touch with the whole range of their feelings, and a little more able to access dual brain hemispheres so they can think and feel at the same time more fluently.

That covers the when. Now for the what. What do you say in response?

Generally, not much… That's the short answer.

A MM is interested in hearing two things from you in a first response email:

1. Did you like what he sent you?
2. Is it a yes or a no in letting him move this forward?

Sending him a short reply that states your position on those two things, in language that he understands, is the task at hand.

Regarding #1 – Did you like what he sent you? Always respond with a positive comment about the note that he sent: *"I enjoyed hearing from you,"* or *"That was a fun email,"* or *"Your note made me smile."* Not juicy enough are responses like: *"Thank you for your note"* or *"I appreciate your interest."* Why? Because pretty much everything that these guys do is done to increase your joy, comfort, relaxation, or safety, and using words like "enjoy" and "fun" and "smile" actually give him a visual of having hit the mark. Thanks and appreciation are nice, but the inference with *"Thank you for your note,"* or *"I appreciate your interest"* is that he did something *right*, rather than something that *lit you up*. We prefer lit you up to right for two reasons:

- He's not in this thing to do things correctly. He's in it to make you happy.
- If you start from the beginning letting him know what's *right*, it implies that what's *wrong* is around the corner, and he knows that he'll eventually hear about it. This is not the conversation that interests him.

Regarding #2 – Are you interested in letting him move this forward: A simple *"You seem like an interesting man. It would be fun to hear from you again,"* is plenty.

Here are two caveats to consider.

First Caveat

If he has proposed something specific, like *"May I call you sometime?"* or *"Would you like to get together for a drink?"* a response is warranted. If you like his idea, let him know: *"I like your idea of a phone call,"* or *"A drink sounds fun. What did you have in mind?"*

If you don't want to do what he's suggested, let him know your positive response to his offering, and then tell him what you would prefer: *"Gosh, a call sounds lovely, but I'd feel most comfortable with a little more email contact. What do you think?"* or *"I enjoy going out for drinks, however I feel like I'd prefer a phone call before we meet. What are your thoughts?"*

You'll notice that three things are going on in my last set of responses. This is important.

1. First, I let him know that I like his idea. So even though I'm not going to take him up on it at this time, he still feels like he's succeeded in pleasing me. *"Gosh, a call sounds lovely..."*

2. Secondly, I let him know clearly, in feminine language, what I'd prefer: *"but I'd feel most comfortable with a little more email contact."* Men like it when women tell them what they want, clearly, as long as it feels like a good-natured request instead of an expectation or demand. Use words like *"sounds lovely," "feel most comfortable,"* or *"enjoy going out."* These are softer, more feminine words. I didn't tell him what to do. Instead I let him know what would make me happy.

3. Thirdly, I capped my redirect by both respecting his thoughts and giving him back the lead. *"What do you think?"*

In a very short note to him I've communicated a lot of information that's important to MMs.

1. What he offered pleased me, be it his note or his bid for further engagement.

2. I find him interesting.

3. It's a "yes" for him to proceed courting me.

4. I am a woman who will tell him what I prefer in a way that enlivens him rather than diminishes him.

Second Caveat

As I said before, MMs often prefer brevity in their initial contacts. They don't like the email medium, and want to get through the perfunctory early contact quickly, ascertain whether or not you're giving him a green light, and, if you are, get to phone and in-person meetings as expediently as possible. But sometimes you will be contacted by a man who will write a longer email. He might resumé for a while, having read your profile and letting you know how he meets your criteria. Or, he might want to give you a stronger sense of who he is to put you at ease. So he'll talk about himself for a while, covering subjects he guesses would be pertinent to you deciding to give him a shot. He might also comment on what you've written about yourself, and ask some questions in order to engage you.

If he's a MM the purpose behind everything that he writes will be the same: *he wants to sell you on the idea of giving him the go ahead to contact you again.*

If you get a longer email, be aware of two things:

First, realize that all you need to do is respond as he has requested, e.g., he may greet you, compliment you, resumé for three paragraphs, and then say, *"So please take a look at my profile and let me know if you're interested."*

You do not need to do anything except tell him, in some form, that you enjoyed his note and learning a little more about him, and that you liked his profile and would welcome hearing from him again. If he asked you specific questions, it's respectful to answer them, briefly, unless the question makes you uncomfortable, in which case simply ignore it. Some women tend to feel that it's either rude to say so little when he said so much, or they feel like they need to respond in kind and get chatty, talk about similar subjects, thank him for his compliments, and ask him questions back in order to get him to like you.

Both are faulty assumptions.

He wrote a long email for one purpose – to get you to say, *"Okay, I'm interested."* When you write back, that's what he's really looking for. He's the one courting you, not vice versa, and he needs to work harder than you in this process. In fact, he doesn't want for you to work *at all* at this stage of the game.

Secondly, the one exception to this principle is if he's talked about the "important" subjects: his work, his dreams, or his family. We'll get into these subjects in more depth in the *How MMs Experience Respect* chapter. However, for our purposes here, if he shares anything about those topics, you want to acknowledge what he shared, and comment, briefly, in a manner that is attentive and respectful.

Example:

He writes:

> "*Hi Cara,*
>
> *I was really impressed by your profile – the thoughtfulness, your ideas and values, and of course you're gorgeous so I had to write!!! You talked about respecting men who dream big and take action to achieve those dreams. I can confidently say that's me. When I was 17 I decided that one day I would become an accomplished mountaineer, and, to date, I've scaled Anapurna 3 times, and I was on one of the first men's teams to take on all of the major South American peaks.*
>
> *Anyway, enough about me. I was wondering if you'd take a look at my profile and let me know if you'd like to talk sometime. I hope so! Have a great day!!!*
>
> *Jack*"

So, noticing the words about his dreams, and exercising the skills from above, you respond:

> "*Hello Jack,*
>
> *It was lovely to hear from you. Wow… You must have had some amazing adventures up in those beautiful mountains. I respect the kind of drive and courage that it takes to fulfill that kind of dream. I read your profile and would enjoy hearing from you again.*
>
> *Cara*"

46

The Graceful No

You need to cut a man loose and say "no." Here's how to do it:

> "Hi Jack,
> I appreciate your sweet note. I don't feel that we're a romantic
> match, but I wish you well.
> Cara"

Appreciate his attempt to connect. Use the word "feel" rather than the word "think" when you say that you're not a match. A man may question or argue with your thoughts, but not with your feelings, unless he's a NAT.

MMs understand that you feel it or you don't. As long as you're respectful and kind when you let him go, he'll move on with dignity. A lot of times these men will actually write back to say thank you for letting them know where you stand. These are good guys, and I think it's exceptionally good karma to leave a trail of well-respected men as you move down this path.

47

Party Talk

Sometimes you'll receive a confusing email.

1. It might be a short, semi-assumptive question like:
   "How's your day going?" or
   "How's this site treating you?" or
   "How come you've never been married?"

2. It might be a brief, non-directive statement like:
   "Nice pics." or
   "So you used to live in Hawaii. Aloha." or
   "I used to have a '59 Chevy pick-up, too."

3. And then there are the short, semi-assumptive, directive statements like:
   "We should have coffee sometime." or
   "You should be a model." or
   "I'll be in town in August. I could use a tour guide."

4. And lastly, there are the longer, slightly confusing missives, like:
   "A woman who loves dogs. Dog people rule." or
   "So you went to UCLA. Go Bruins! I'm a USC man myself." or
   "A piece of poetry... (insert poem.)"

Here are a few thoughts on these obtuse communications.

Biggest Principle: You never have to do anything that feels uncomfortable, and you never have to respond to anything that doesn't feel good. If you feel confused, or don't want to answer him, do nothing. Re-vet his profile. If he seems masculine and his words feel benign, albeit clueless, just let the email sit in your inbox without a response. See if he figures it out and decides to man-up a little more later. You're waiting for him to show himself and make a move. Give him a little time to turn it around.

If he doesn't seem masculine, or the email feels creepy, just delete it.

If, however, you kinda like him, and you want to respond, I suggest that you employ something that I call "Party Talk." Here's how it works: if a man you didn't know came up to you at a party and said the words this guy wrote in his email, what would you say in response?

(Him) *"How's your day going?"*
(You) *"Great, thanks…"*

(Him) *"You should be a model."*
(You) *"That's sweet. Thanks…"*

(Him) *"I saw you drove a '59 Chevy. I used to have one, too."*
(You) *"Cool…"*

You can respond to him just like that, except you'll put a full 24 hours in between his note and your response. No need to say more in order to try and engage him. Just relax and respond, in kind, to what he offers.

Like that.

Remember that NATs want you off balance, so if you're self-esteem is tanking, or you're second-guessing yourself in response to his note, get out of there and delete him. But if your gut is relaxed, just party talk a bit. Keep up the banter and see where it goes.

48

More About How MMs Resumé for You

Remember that they read your profile like a job description, and the job is this: *making you happy and getting a shot at increasing your joy, comfort, relaxation, and safety.* They provide, protect, and cherish – it's who they are and it's what they're wired to do. If you present yourself as a woman who is available for cherishing, chances are men will apply for the job. Once he's ascertained that he would be a good candidate, he'll read your profile to get clues about how to do the job, looking for things that you enjoy, what makes you happy, and what you like to do for fun. And he'll also read about what kind of men you like. In his initial (and sometimes subsequent) emails he may then do some lobbying on his own behalf, in the form of referring to what you said in your profile and commenting on how he can provide the things you like, and how he's the kind of man that you said that you preferred.

> *"Hey Alana,*
> *It was a joy to read your profile and see your beautiful face. I noticed that you said that you enjoy men who make fun plans and take the lead. I think I can confidently say that you're describing me. I'm known among my friends as the man to call for good ideas and I'm great with details and creative adventures. I hope you'll allow me to show you some memorable adventures. Please take a look at my profile, and if you're interested, let's talk.*
> *All the best*
> *Brian"*

"Wow! Sophie, your profile bowled me over. You know, you mentioned that kindness and compassion are the axis on which your world turns. I study compassionate communication, and I follow the creed of kindness to all creatures. I'd love to take you to lunch and we could talk more about this. Would you like that?
Hope to hear from you
Ralph"

I find it endearing when men resumé. There's often an openness with which they go after letting you know just why they might deserve that shot at getting to know you. And because most MMs are fairly experienced at selling themselves in the workplace, and their self-esteem is generally high, they can take rejection with a great attitude and move on, especially if they feel like they represented themselves well, and, again, you were kind as you said "no."

49

A Word About Compliments

In this second section of *Absolutely Adored* we've been looking at creating profiles and vetting the suitors who contact you. As we segue into phone calls and in-person dates, I'd like to touch on a few ideas in these next four chapters that will be key principles as you start to move off the page and into real time with your men.

When MMs give to you or provide for you, they want evidence that they have succeeded in achieving their primary purpose, increasing your:
- happiness
- comfort
- safety
- relaxation

When they receive that evidence in language or behavior that they understand, they feel fulfilled and energized to give or provide more. This successful dynamic is one of the key components in allowing MMs to fall in love.

Feminine women, on the other hand, are on the road to falling in love when they repeatedly receive that which allows them to experience an increase in their happiness, comfort, safety, and/or relaxation. As I have spoken about earlier in this book, women become depleted from too much giving, whereas MMs become vitalized from giving when their giving hits the mark.

So when you compliment a MM, in general what he is looking for is an *indirect compliment:* that is, a statement of appreciation that clearly and directly lets him know that you feel good *as a result of what he has given, who he is, and what he does.* They do not respond as well to direct compliments: telling them what's so great about *them.*

Let's say he's taking you out to dinner. He wants to hear:
"Wow, what a beautiful restaurant. I love it here."
Or
"This fish is so exquisite. Yum. You have to have a bite."
Or
"I can't tell you how relaxing this is for me to just sit back and enjoy a quiet, wonderful meal after this busy week."
(All of the above are indirect compliments.)

Much less potent for him is:
"You're so smart for deciding on this restaurant."
Or
"You suggest the fish? Good choice."
Or
"You were really intuitive in deciding to take me out to dinner tonight."
(All of the second responses were direct compliments.)

MMs aren't vain, so they don't really groove on hearing how great they are, like a more narcissistic man would, unless the statement about their greatness *is followed by another statement that tells them how their coolness makes your life and your feelings better.*

> *"You're so smart for choosing this restaurant. I **love** this place."*
> *"Great choice suggesting the fish. Yum. This is the **best** salmon I've ever had."*
> *"You're a pretty intuitive guy in deciding to take me out to dinner tonight. I had a really demanding week at work, and it feels **so good** to just relax in this beautiful place with great food and great company."*

Get the sense of this?

(Caveat: I'm not saying that a well-placed, *"Hi handsome,"* or *"My boyfriend is a genius,"* isn't appreciated every now and then. For sure they like those kind of affectionate and appreciative direct compliments, especially when it's obvious that you *feel good* about him when you say it. It's just all about how you feel, and him being able to comprehend that who he is or what he's done *is the source of your feel-good*.)

Feminine women like direct compliments. We enjoy being fluffed up with appreciation for our beauty and brains, right? I mean, we work hard to look great, and it feels good to get pretty for our guy, and we like for someone to notice our strong points and assets. I don't know about you, but when I spend an hour or so getting ready for a date, and the guy does not say word one about how beautiful I am, it's definitely a downer. And, conversely, when a man compliments me – my looks, my ideas or creations, my nature – I feel good. I relax, I feel more confident and happy, and I blossom.

A strange caveat: Some men actually believe that it is "cheesy" to tell a woman that she is beautiful. I suggest that you really let your men know that you enjoy their compliments when they give them. Here are some suggestions for how to do that:

He says *"Wow, you look gorgeous!"*
You smile and say, *"Mmmmm... that feels good."*
or *"Thank you. I like it when you say things like that."*
or *"You know how to make me feel good."*
or *"I love it when you notice and let me know."*

So, he likes to know that your well-being is increased by what he does, who he is, and what he provides, and you like to know that he thinks that you're a goddess.

We'll refer to these kinds of compliments in future chapters.

50

A Word About Complaints

Alison Armstrong teaches women that men are not "big, hairy, defective women," and that if we treat them like they are, nobody wins.

One of the ways that I see women behaving as if men are, indeed, big hairy, defective women is when they assume that men and women feel and think alike. And in the area of complaining, this can come up a lot.

Women are used to telling each other *everything*. One of the ways that we can bond with each other is by talking about the hard stuff. Sometimes women who barely know each other establish a rapport and begin to discuss difficult situations in their lives, and both talk about, and listen to, that kind of material with openness and compassion. It can feel pretty good.

I'm not advocating for bonding through the wound. I'm just saying that women can go there with each other pretty easily.

Not so with guys.

In my years of coaching I have repeatedly found that MMs feel pain more acutely than most women – physical pain and emotional pain. And when their woman is in distress, they feel that distress acutely. In her wonderful book, "*The Happiness Project*," author Gretchen Rubin has a section called "*No Dumping*" in the chapter about improving her marriage. She relates a story about asking her husband why he isn't more receptive when she wants to talk about the hard things in her life, and he says:

"I just can't stand to see you unhappy."

That's the deal. MMs are compelled to increase your well-being, and when you talk about things that are challenges that he cannot fix, he hurts. This is not to say that these guys have no capacity to hear about those kinds of challenges. But, especially in the early stages of dating, they need to succeed a lot at fulfilling their primary drive, making you feel good, and if you talk about the hard stuff early on, it puts a drag on his courtship momentum. In the first three stages of dating, he needs to build up a storehouse of experiences where he succeeds in increasing your well-being – he's with a woman who is happy, often and obviously. Once he's become convinced that he's a guy who could really make life good for you in the long run, he'll have more stamina for the unsolvable challenges that show up later.

Women who are encouraged to put their best foot forward and present the most optimistic aspects of themselves in early dating sometimes grossly misunderstand the principle behind this suggestion. It's not that you have to be someone that you're not, or that your potency and depth is too much for him – this is **not** why it's best to put your best foot forward in the beginning. The reason why it's best to primarily present the optimistic aspects of yourself at this stage is so that he experiences success with you. This success is something that takes a while to build and cultivate. If you show the depth of your bigger problems, he'll hurt for you.

Unfortunately, most high performance women are fairly uncomfortable *not* going deep, fast. And when women go too deep, too fast, chances are they will recoil a little down the line. The recoil is a result of having skipped vital stages in the getting-to-know-you process, and, consequently, women find themselves too intimate, too soon, with a guy they may not actually like. So rather than risk the vulnerability of taking it slow and steady, high-performance gals often let it all hang out, right from the gate. And then, when he becomes discouraged and backs off, that kind of woman will say to herself (and anyone else who will listen), *"Oh well, another guy who couldn't handle the real me."*

If she had moved a little more slowly, she would have built a foundation of optimism and joy that would allow her man to develop the necessary confidence and stamina regarding his ability to make her happy. Without those building blocks, he's often left feeling like he's suddenly whipping around a skyscraper of issues that he can't provision. He needs a backlog of experiences successfully and consistently lighting up his woman before he can handle the issues that he can't fix. If a woman's intensity hits him all at once, early on, he'll start feeling like a failure and probably leave. Those are the romantic mechanics of what happens if a woman shares too much of herself in the beginning.

Understand this very vital difference between men and women and you'll be able to exercise some discretion about how, when, and what you share with compassion, rather than feeling like it's one more cheesy dating rule. This knowledge will stay with you for the duration of your relationship, and serve you well.

51

Wearing the Wound

I like to use this phrase to describe the excessive need to define needs or boundaries in people's online profiles in a manner that clearly refers to some past pain. For example, if you have been cheated on by past partners, perhaps you stress that you need someone who is loyal and puts the relationship first. Or, if you have been with people who are very needy, maybe you state that you clearly want someone who has their own life and interests, and who is independent and autonomous. Or you may have been with people who used you financially, and so you make it clear that you want a partner who has his or her own money and is financially secure.

None of these needs are wrong, and speaking about them and clarifying them in a profile is not bad. The issue is that there can be a push behind the way that those needs are expressed that feels like you have not resolved the past wound, so you are preemptively guarding against it happening again. It's a kind of announcement that says, *"Don't be like her, or him, and I'll be on guard with you until you prove that you aren't."* It speaks to the probability that the writer may have generalized the issue (all men are selfish and untrustworthy, all women are changeable and disloyal), instead of taking responsibility for healing their own part in the problem from the past, and then proceeding with a softer and healthier walk into the future.

I mention this here both so that you can be aware of this when you construct your profile, and you can also notice when potential suitors are wearing *their* wounds.

52

Bonding Through the Wound

It's what happens when we talk about the hard stuff, early on: childhood issues, medical problems, difficult relationship experiences, etc. It's a way of creating connection, sometimes deep connection, through a *"Yeah, I know what you mean 'cause I've been there, too"* mentality. Sometime it can become our primary means of relating and feeling close. It's not bad. It's just not where we want to go in the early stages of dating, as I've previously discussed.

If you have habitually engaged in bonding through the wound as a way to create intimacy, it may feel unnatural to shy away from those behaviors and focus on lighter aspects of yourself and your life. Give it a little time and practice. The rewards are worth the effort.

53

Regarding Phone Calls

Maybe you're expecting his call at a certain time, so you know that you have the space to relax and sink into your feminine. But then again, maybe his call comes unexpectedly, and you're in the car, or busy and engaged with some timelines at home. I suggest that you begin to experiment with how quickly you can relax and tune into your sensuality and enjoyment so that you can move into your feminine efficiently, should you be surprised by his contact. An upcoming chapter, *Feminine Rituals*, is a comprehensive guide to that shift.

When you know that he's going to call, plan on 10 to 15 minutes on the phone. Make sure you relax and transition into your feminine energy before the phone call. Allow yourself to be present, and intend to enjoy the experience. Remember that you're going to stay on the most optimistic side of any given subject. As much as you can, allow him to lead. Let him start the conversation and, hopefully, ask the first questions. He may be nervous since he is going out on a limb to call a woman that he is interested in, so he may sound awkward. Your job is to breathe and relax, and let him have his experience.

Because of that awkwardness he may ask you a general question like *"How was your day?"* or *"So how are you?"* Whatever the question, just remember to stay in optimism and joy. In terms of the ratio of give and take, I would lean toward one question from you to his every two.

If you're enjoying yourself, stay on the phone for about 12 minutes, and then say to him, *"I'm enjoying this call, and I'm going to need to go in a few minutes."* Then be quiet, and breathe, and allow him to switch brain hemispheres. You'll know he's transitioning from feeling to thinking because he'll make noises that sound like, *"Oh, a few minutes, oh, uh...*" He may become quiet for a few seconds. Eventually he will have an organized thought, e.g., *"Would you like to do this again?"* or *"Can I take you out next weekend?"*

If you know that you'd like for things to continue, say yes. If he asks you if you'd like another phone call, go ahead and set one up. If he asks you if you'd like to get together in person, for coffee, or lunch, or another date, and you want to do it, just make sure the date is at least three days later, and preferably five or six. If he offers something general, like, *"Would you like to get together sometime?"* encourage him to be more specific by saying something like, *"Getting together might be fun. What did you have in mind?"*

Every time he has to get specific with a plan, it encourages him to work. And working for what he's trying to earn, which in this case is time with you, will allow him to become energized by the task at hand. (I want to be clear that when I talk about encouraging or allowing him to work, I'm referring to the work that is his to do, e.g., calling you, courting you, caring about you. I am not insinuating that you throw up artificial road blocks so that he'll need to prove that he is working.)

Remember that masculine men fall in love when they give, so you don't do him any favors when you try and make things easy for him in the beginning. Plus, courtship is about him wooing you for the purpose of winning you. So let him.

54

First Phone Calls with Long Distance Suitors

First phone calls are first dates with a long-distance suitor. Consequently, they will be longer and have more substance than first phone calls with men who are local. The phone calls with local men are a way for you to get a sense of whether or not you'd like to meet them, so they are short and light, and you're scanning for courting dynamics.

But talking with a man who is geographically distant is a different story. You will put on your feminine and check out his masculine. You will ask each other more questions, and have an opportunity to listen well.

I suggest that you plan anywhere from 20 to 40 minutes for the initial call. I also suggest that you make a strong, conscious shift into your feminine energy before the call. I actually prepare for one of these calls like I would for an in-person date. I bathe and dress nicely, and put on makeup and perfume. I consciously relax. I want to be sitting back into my *feel-good* by the time that phone rings.

You'll know pretty quickly whether you're comfortable with him, and whether or not you'd like to talk for a while. If you want to stay on the phone, breathe a lot, ask him about his work, family, etc. It's not a bad idea to have a copy of his profile and pics in front of you so that you can refer to them.

End the call as you would with a local suitor, and give him space to decide what happens next.

Have fun. Use the upcoming first date guidelines as an additional reference point.

55

Falling in Love by Email or Phone

It's easy to see how you might become infatuated with a man who is courting you well in his initial emails. If he is cherishing, funny, insightful, and reliable, and if he is studying your happiness, it's delightful and intoxicating. He might be asking you great questions and be attentive to your answers. He might be offering parts of himself that are endearing and nurturing. He might be fulfilling some emotional needs that you have for empathy, or fun, or connection. I have found that it's best not to prolong the email relationship past two or three exchanges. If you are vetting well, and have ascertained that he is probably masculine by examining both his correspondence and his profile, I suggest that you move it along to either a phone call or meeting for coffee. Even if he is far away geographically, the sooner you meet, the better. It's tempting to project when your only contact is by email. And even the phone leaves room for the imagination.

Early on in my online dating experience I interacted with a man who lived several states away and it was almost six weeks before we met. During that time we had quite a bit of contact both by mail and by phone, and I found myself falling in love with who I thought he was. When we met, the chemistry was not there, and it was very difficult to let go of my fantasy of who I had hoped we might be together. I have had clients who have experienced the same thing. So just be aware when that oxytocin starts kicking in right at the beginning, and back it up with the next level of contact. You won't know about the sustainable chemistry until you meet in person.

56

First Date Preparation

As with all phases of this process, the focus here is on showing up in your feminine and allowing the man to court you. You get to practice staying in your self-love, and inherent, feminine fabulousness, relaxing, and continuing to present the most optimistic aspects of yourself. You also get to practice giving him chasing space, and allowing him to be "the guy" while enjoying yourself.

Energetic Preparation

This is the time to really increase and acquaint yourself with the personal rituals that will help create an energetic bridge from your daily life into your feminine. (See the next chapter, "*Feminine Rituals*," for in-depth practices.) For some women that might mean a hot bath with candles and bath salts, or filling your house with fresh flowers, or walking barefoot out in the grass, drinking in the beauty of nature. For others, it might mean taking a long time to prepare and dress and do your makeup, or putting on some music that connects you with that feminine essence and dancing. It's for you to become a student of what aids you in making the transition from more masculine "get-it-done" energy into your joyful, sensual receptivity, and then creating whatever rituals you need, and can do, to make the shift. You want to be relaxed, feeling beautiful and valuable, and quite in love with yourself by the time you and your date intersect. Being in love with yourself will put a smile on your face.

Clothes, Hair, Makeup, Perfume

You want to look good, smell good, sound good, and (when appropriate) taste good.

I really encourage you to wear dresses or skirts and attractive tops when you can. Masculine men feel gifted when a woman wears a dress, especially if her legs and/or arms show, somewhat.

As in the photos for your profile (if you are online dating), brighter colors around your face are great: your version of reds, corals, burgandys, blues. Skin is sensual, so as much neck and chest as you are comfy exposing is beautiful to these men. We're not going for trashy, but, instead, sexy and occasion-appropriate. Clothes that are a little more form-fitting, and not boxy, are also beautiful to these guys.

Let your hair be soft around the face, not pulled back tightly in any way. Apply makeup that makes you feel and look soft, vibrant, and approachable.

Delicious smells are big on the list of wonderful things for masculine men. So wear a little perfume or essential oil. Not too much, or too heavy, but something that will linger with him when you're gone.

A man knows when he's with a woman who takes care of herself, and who is presenting herself in her authentic beauty. You don't have to be a movie star to be beautiful in their eyes. Confidence and self-love are very attractive qualities, and as long as you feel good about yourself, you're on strong footing.

57

Feminine Rituals

It's time to be the girl, consciously, intentionally, and undeniably...

At this point, you probably understand that much of what is yours to do as you date will be happening in the realm of your energy and the manner in which you inhabit your body and your emotions. Moving into your feminine energy in order to be able to enjoy, recognize, and receive the masculine is the big-ticket item here.

So many women with full and productive lives can lose touch with the beautiful, multi-layered biosphere that we call our body, and all of its exquisite sensitivities. Too much logical left-brain activity can place women in an energetic whiteout. The repetitive MO of thinking, planning, anticipating the needs of others, and making things happen can result in a state of disconnection with the body, submission to imposed schedules and timelines, and hyper-vigilance.

Magnetism is the unique energetic of women who know and nurture their inherent femininity. It's all about developing an intimate relationship with our own propensity for the feeling realm, sensuality in its purest form. What actually feels good to me, at any given moment? What do I actually enjoy? What do I actually want to do, now, and now, and now? Am I in touch with my body, with my senses, with my instincts, with my natural rhythms?

Most of us understand the concept of personal power and enlivenment as a function of focus and output, and we're good at it. We know how to pony up and put out with style, balance, organization, and graciousness. That's good. That's great. But at the end of the day, I know that I'm not interested in meeting my date and doing more of the same. I'm depleted and want to have him "cashmere me." I need some yummy cherishing, and I need to be able to take it in. Count on it.

If I don't take the time to transition from She-Who-Could-Run-the-World to She-Who-is-Relaxed-and-Receptive before I spend time with Mr. Possibly Wonderful, there's a good chance I won't have as much fun, and enjoy as high a level of courtship as I might wish.

As you switch into dating mode, it's helpful to build some bridges that help you move from that more masculine energy into your feminine energy – bridges that are reliable, sometimes expedient, and always available. Let's call those bridges *"the shift."*

Relaxation is one of the most immediately recognizable signs that you're making *the shift*. Increased sensuality is another. Diffused focus is good. Sense of humor is good. Emotional awareness is key. High self-esteem is pivotal, and self-love is the center of the circle.

Recognizing the qualities of feminine energy, here are a few key principles and tools that will aid you in making *the shift*, followed by some specific ideas and actions that might become part of your toolkit.

1. *Awareness:* If this were the only principle you remembered, it would reap many rewards. *Be aware that you need to make the shift.* Recognize that you've been *in the masculine*, and before you interact with potential suitors, you can choose to move your energy into the feminine.

2. *Viability:* Given where you've been and what comes next, in terms of your time and energy, what are some realistic ways that you can relax and tune into your feelings and body? When you plan dates, remember that you need a cushion of time before you meet to release drive, competition, people-pleasing, and accommodating others in favor of self-focus, pleasure, and fun.

3. *Choices:* Play around with different methods of shifting. Become a student of your own pleasure and comfort. Find out what takes

you where you want to go. Be creative. Keep experimenting and realize that you can keep updating and learning.

4. *Writing:* Keep a running journal of the activities, focuses, and practices that help you sink in and get your woman on. Notate what kind of time you need for each in order to achieve maximum feminine potency.

5. *Touchstones:* Notice what kind of "cues" you can keep around your personal spaces that create an instant shift: the sight of fresh flowers, the sound of running water, the fragrance of certain perfumes or oils. Perhaps you have some art that takes you into your subjective right brain: images, textures, colors, smells. What does it for you? Make a point of infusing your home, your office, and your car with some of these cues so that you have feminine touchstones readily available.

6. *Intention:* Intend to remember to shift. Men need transition time and so do you. Enlist your angels to help you. Use the power of your consciousness on your own behalf.

7. *Make the list:* An exercise that I particularly like is telling myself why I'm such a great catch: *"I'm beautiful, my smile is contagious, my capacity for pleasure is huge, I have a laugh like a Montana ranch hand, I have a wicked sense of humor, my touch is sensual and healing, etc., etc., etc."* If I put on some confectionery lingerie, and speak my list out loud at the same time, with *"Sexual Healing"* by Marvin Gaye playing in the background, I am well on my way to embodying my receptive, soft, sexy me.

8. *Breathe, breathe, breathe:* And while you breathe, relax the jaw, the back of the neck, the brain, and the pelvis. Throughout the day take little breathing breaks to thaw out and connect with your body.

9. *Belly/brain:* While breathing, imagine your brain sinking down into your belly. Eyes soften, extremities feeling their blood flow, and belly brain. Try walking through small sections of

your day thinking from belly/brain and check out where that takes you.

10. *Nature contact:* Take a walk in some beautiful nature and notice her rhythms – the way the breeze rustles the leaves, the sound and frequency of bird songs, the movement of the clouds. Let yourself take a ride on those rhythms, while breathing and relaxing. Sometimes just a few minutes of connection with undomesticated reality can reboot our sensuality, light-heartedness, and softness.

Here are more suggestions for building your feminine bridge. Add your creative ideas to this list.

- Yoga or stretching
- Hot baths with bath salts or fragrant oils
- Any physical workout that you enjoy
- Meditation and prayer
- Fun talks with galpals
- Dancing naked
- Listening to great music
- Fragrances that are yummy: fresh flowers, perfume or essential oils, certain foods (One of my clients has a bottle of a particular men's cologne. When she takes a whiff, it engages her feminine very quickly.)
- The feel of certain textures
- Eat a sensual snack in a sensual way. Ladies, you know what I mean. Play with it.
- Naps
- Listen to the sound of his voice on your voicemail
- Love your body
- Fresh flowers
- Walk barefoot in the grass

- Watch the clouds and breathe
- Get a facial or a massage
- Laugh – really laugh from your gut
- Create
- Sing
- Look at reminders of those who love and adore you
- Positive affirmations
- Loving self-talk
- Let your hair down
- Practice gratitude
- Focus on what's beautiful in your immediate surroundings
- (You make it up)

Find your way, find your flavor, and let the gushy goodness of your pleasure-focused, sensual fluency take center stage. Then, when you meet him, you'll have your soft on, and there will be an automatic atmosphere of cherishing around you, because *you put it in place.*

58

First Date Guidelines

Keep it short, meet during the day, and let him pay. Coffee's good. An hour to an hour and fifteen minutes is a great amount of time. If you are really enjoying yourself, you can push it to an hour and a half. You want to see him in an atmosphere that's casual and public, yet quiet enough that you can have some clear conversation. Even though it might be fun to meet for a drink in the evening and get a little more dressed up, evening dates can start to trigger oxytocin in some women, and you need to have your head on straight. Please do not veer in the direction of taking a hike or a long walk. That may put you in a position where you're alone with him, which is not good for several reasons.

One: you may not like him, and you can't make an easy getaway.

Two: it's not as safe as a public venue.

Three: sometimes hikes stretch into more than an hour, and he needs some chasing space.

Four: when you're in a place where he has an opportunity, right off, to provide financially by buying your coffee or tea, you get some needed information immediately. By this I mean if he easily and naturally pays for your drink, great. If he wants to go dutch, or leaves you to your own devices to order and pay for coffee, you're getting immediate information about either his bank account or the level of his generosity.

During the date practice the skills you've been learning for phone contact, and translate them to the in person venue: smile, breathe, let him be the guy, let him start and lead the conversation and questions, laugh, enjoy yourself in his presence, obey your sense of comfort. This is a great time to feel for initial chemistry, gather some data about his personal presentation, and ask him questions about his work, lifestyle, dreams, and family. This is not the time to get into painful subjects, or disclose deeper, personal material.

It's important that you get your "girl on," so that you're in touch with yourself and your comfort level. For example, you never need answer questions that don't feel good. You can steer the conversation away from topics that you don't want to talk about. And you can engage with topics that allow you to feel relaxed and comfortable. This is one of the reasons why it's so important to be in touch with your body and emotions before you arrive. If you're not in touch with yourself, it will be difficult to tell how you feel when you're with him.

If he asks you about something that makes you uneasy, say, past relationships, or your experience online, or something personal – all you have to do is *stroke and stand*. That means that you thank him for the desire to know about you, and then let him know what you'd prefer.

"I appreciate your interest (stroke), *and I'm not comfortable talking about that right now* (stand)."

Or you can give him a brief, general answer and redirect.

"I am really blessed to have been with some wonderful men in my life. You mentioned that you were thinking about going back to school. What is it that you want to study?"

If there is silence in the conversation, breathe and smile. If, for any reason, you feel uncomfortable and no longer want to be there, e.g., he is flirting with the waitress, he makes a remark that you find offensive, or he's complacent or rude, you can get up, say, *"I'm leaving now,"* and walk. If things are going well and you stay, at around an hour say, *"I'm really enjoying being with you, and I'm going to need to go in a few minutes."* Same ending behavior that you exercise on the phone: wait, smile. As you probably experienced on the phone, you'll hear him switch brain hemispheres. Let him. Don't talk. He will come up with what's next. If he wants to see you again, he'll make that known.

"Um, uh, oh, a few minutes… Would you like to get together again?" or *"Would you like to go out for dinner next week?"* or *"That movie you said you liked is playing. Would you like to get a bite to eat and see it next Saturday?"*

If you're not sure that you want to see him, or you know that you don't, but you don't want to say that right then, say, *"Oh, that might be fun. Can I let you know in a few days? I'd like to go home and sort out how I feel after a first date."*

Shake his hand and be on your way. Give it a few days and then write your graceful decline if you don't want to get together again.

If you know that you *do* want to see him, and he proposes the next date, it's fine to say yes, for example, *"Yes, the movie sounds fun,"* or *"I'd love to go to dinner next week."*

If his proposal was vague, for example, *"Would you like to get together again?"* ask him to specify. Say, *"That might be fun. What are you thinking?"* He may be unable to think clearly because he's liking you. He will probably respond by either coming up with a plan right then, *"Oh – are you free next Saturday for a movie?"* or he will buy some time. *"Well, how about if I call you Monday with some ideas. When are you free next week?"* Put a good five days in between the two dates, and give him a few options for when you will be available. He will probably walk you to your car. Let him. Give him a little hug, say farewell.

If he doesn't want to see you again, he will say something like, *"Well, it's been nice to meet you."* Game over.

Do not send him a thank you note, which may be hard to do if you liked him. It is on him to follow up with appreciation for spending time with *you*. If he was vague about the details of the next date, expect him to contact you when he said he would with some plans. When he does, let him lead. Unless what he proposes is not possible or offensive, be appreciative and roll with it. Second dates can be a little longer, especially if part of it is a shared activity that you're doing together without having to be face-to-face, such as dinner, where you *are* face-to-face for an hour or so, and then a movie, or music, or a lecture. So maybe three to four hours if it's a double activity, or two hours, max, if it's a meal. You don't have to tell him about those time constraints. Just don't agree to anything longer, for example a day trip to the wine country, or a long hike, etc.

Take a little time to love yourself up for doing so well up to now. Good job!

59
First Date Follow-up

Okay. Pretty good experience with the first date. If you're not going to move forward with a man who had expressed interest in wanting to see you again, and you weren't clear at the end of the first date that you were *not* going to see him again, send him a little email that says, *"Thank you for coffee yesterday. After thinking about it, I don't feel that we're a romantic match, so I will forgo getting together again. All the best."* MMs understand chemistry. They do not take it personally if a woman does not *feel* the romantic spark. They appreciate the clear communication, and they let go.

If you *do* want to see him again, and he moved things in that direction, you will hopefully receive an email, text, or call from him within 24 hours of the first date letting you know that he had a good time, and that you were wonderful. Again, this is his job, not yours.

If you do not hear from him within 24 hours, or he doesn't contact you when he said he would, take note. You need men who are reliable, and who take a strong, secure lead in courtship.

Having said that, I like to give everyone a chance to blow it, once. And I also like to give guys the benefit of the doubt, once. Maybe his work suddenly became intense. Maybe a pressing personal or family issue came up. So I would wait a week. If you still haven't heard from him, I would do what I call "putting a tack on his chair." Send him a little note that says:

"Hi _____ (his name),
Hoping you had a great week. Mine was wonderful.
All the best
_____ (your name)"

Here's what you're doing, and why: Because MMs are single-focused, if something comes along that demands his full attention, he'll forget about everything else, including you, until the issue at hand is resolved. Then, when he remembers you, especially if he liked you and wanted to ask you out again, he'll think that he blew it by not getting back to you sooner. His natural instinct is to avoid your anger, so he just disappears. By sending him the tack, you're saying in language that he understands, *"I'm not mad. I'd love to hear from you again."* He'll usually respond very quickly.

If you like this guy then it's all the more important that you are simultaneously dating a few other men. The old model would be to invest quickly in one guy, give too much too fast, and you know the rest by now. The new model is several men, simultaneously, slowly, in small increments, with some space in between.

Slow, slow, slow, keep it light, and diversify.

60

I Had No Idea

This is the happy exclamation that I often hear from clients who are discovering that what I'm teaching is true. Generous cherishing men do exist, in abundance, and when they start shining their light on you, it's a whole, new, glorious world.

61

Second Date Guidelines

So things went well enough to warrant a second date, and he has put that in motion. Now the fun can start.

This is the moment to turn up the heat with a longer transition time, some deeper feminine rituals, and a chance to play dress-up. Enjoy it. Savor it. You are resuscitating your feminine and giving her some running room, and the preparation is wonderful. If he appreciates you when he sees you, and lets you know it, great. If the date goes well, and another date is planned, great. But let the preparation be its own delicious interlude.

Because what is really happening here? You have vetted this man through emails, maybe a phone call and a first meeting, and he has been granted admission to the dance. You are both in far enough to actually be exploring one another for a possible relationship later. Or, even though you think there won't be a relationship down the line, you have decided to practice dating with a masculine man. And the way this part of the exploring happens is by focusing on fun. Whoo hoo!

So go ahead and play some soulful, sexy music, and bathe, and coif, and do makeup, and dress, and look great, and smell good. Be your beautiful self. Remember that he's in this for a great date with a beautiful woman, so don't stop from giving him your beauty, even if you think, up front, that there won't be much future with him.

This deal is about receiving, and that's what you're preparing for: receiving his appreciation, and maybe compliments, receiving his attention and attentiveness, receiving his chivalry, receiving the experience, the meal, the movie, the event that he is providing.

If you are not so good at receiving, now is the time to practice, because, on a second date, that's how you give back. Don't pick up your purse when the check arrives. Don't feel like you have to reciprocate by making him dinner next time. Just enjoy, and receive, and relax, and let him fluff you up. Your enjoyment, your smile and laughter, your smiling "*Thank you*" when he compliments you, or pulls out your chair, or pays for the meal – that's your contribution.

Really.

If you have any resistance to receiving, and continuing to receive, look at your list and remind yourself why you're such a great catch. Also remember that, unlike women, these gentlemen like to give, and they get off on your delight. They are not depleted by giving, as we often are. They are energized by it, as long as it hits the mark.

If he's picking you up at your house or apartment, be ready when he gets there. It's fine to invite him in for a moment while you gather yourself together. Smile a lot. If you want to have some light physical contact like a hug or a little peck on the cheek, that's great. Let him attend to you by helping you on with your coat and opening the doors: car doors, restaurant doors. If, for some reason, he doesn't open doors for you, just stand next to the door and don't touch it. Even if you walk out to the car and he goes around to the driver side and gets in, just stand there. He'll look over, wonder what's keeping you, and then, "ding!" The bell goes off in his head, and he realizes *he's* the guy, and *you're* the girl, and you're on a *date!* He'll get out, come around, and open the door for you. You get in, smile, say, "*Thank you*," and exhale.

And then, when you arrive, just sit there and breathe until he walks around and opens that door again. Again smile, "*Thank you*." Breathe. And then do the same thing at the door to the restaurant or other venue. Don't help him out. *Maybe*, at some point down the road, when you've been dating a while, and you're in your grubbies, and you're going out to the woods for a long hike, *maybe* you'll open the door and get in that truck when his arms are full of the picnic gear and the walking sticks and the blanket. *Maybe*. But when you're just getting to know each other, and you're dressed up, it's his great pleasure to honor you.

Remember that women teach men how to treat them. Strong lesson right here.

You might be thinking, *"OMG! Really? That takes a lot of nerve and a lot of breathing."* True. But if you can, try it. My experience is that there are definitive moments in the process of really discovering the scope of how MMs give, and this is one of them. If you did this door business with a NAT, he would make you pay dearly for it. And that's probably who you've been with in the past, and probably what you expect or project. But chivalrous MMs shine when they have a gracious queen on whom they can attend. It makes him a bigger man when he's with a fully feminine woman. So, again, give it a try.

If, indeed, he is driving you to this date, know that while he is actually driving, he will probably stay single-focused, with that focus being to transport and deliver his precious cargo – that would be you – safely and expediently. This means that conversation is not a high priority for him, or maybe even possible. If you talk, keep it light, and don't expect for him to remember what you talked about. Once you've arrived, and he's got you seated and comfortable, you can expect him to become more relational again.

Another FYI: if he is driving, let him drive, and, unless he's asked you to, don't navigate. If he's going the wrong way, or missed the exit, or you spot a great parking place, keep it to yourself. Let him make his own mistakes, or do it his way. And if he remarks at some point later about how he should've taken a different exit or gone another way, don't chime in with the fact that you noticed that. Just leave it alone. When you've been seeing him for a while, if you spot a pattern of him consistently getting lost, or not navigating well, you might ask him if he would like your assistance in that arena.

Maybe.

Later.

Part of what you're learning on this date is whether or not you like his lead. *So you have to let him exercise it*, and see how it goes.

Your job is receptivity, and learning to enjoy, and get comfortable with, receiving.

If he is not picking you up for this date, go ahead and be a few minutes late meeting him – a few, like five. If, for some reason, he is not there, go for a walk and come back five or ten minutes later. If he has not called or texted you to say that he will be late, don't be there waiting when he arrives. And if he keeps you waiting for more than 15 minutes without communicating, leave. It will be on him to rectify that.

Assuming he's there, have fun. Give him lots of indirect compliments: *"Oh, I love this place. The lighting is so beautiful." "This feels so good to just relax and have a nice meal. What a treat." "Yum, it's hard to decide what to order. Everything looks so good."*

Let him take you in. He's paying particular attention to your eyes and smile, so share them.

Really this date sets the scene for future dates. He's providing, you're receiving and enjoying, and you're practicing being the girl and letting him be the guy. Remember, keep it to a couple of hours if it's a meal, and three or four hours if it's a meal and an activity, such as a movie or a walk.

The check: my friend Michael, a very masculine man, says, *"Any seventh grader knows that if you ask her out, you pay for the date."*

When that check comes, as I mentioned before, don't go for your purse, don't ask him if he'd like for you to split it, don't do anything except smile. MMs will generally grab it as soon as it arrives, and that's that. If he doesn't grab it, or at least move it over to his side of the table, or if the whole thing feels stressful, get up, take your purse, excuse yourself, and go to the ladies' room. Stay there for at least five minutes. Freshen up. Take out your flashcards from my website, if you have them, and read a few. Breathe, and when you're ready, go back and sit down. Usually he will have handled the check by the time you return. If, for some reason, he expects or wants you to contribute, do so, and know that this is his swan song.

I once had a client who was out on a second date – dinner at a nice restaurant. When the check arrived she did nothing, and her guy said something like, *"Aren't you going to offer to pay half?"* She looked at him and smiled and said, *"I would rather sit here all night and watch you wash dishes than even touch my purse."* He loved it, and laughed, and took care of it. This is another example of how we teach men how to treat us.

Dealing, or in this case, *not* dealing with the check is another one of those definitive moments where you learn, in real time, the difference between MMs and NATs.

If you happen to be out with a man who is a little complacent because women have done too much for him, sitting in the car until he comes around and opens the door, or smiling and letting them pay is a huge relief for these guys. They might grumble a little at first, but once they understand what's happening, they tend to bounce right into their full masculine energy with lots of enthusiasm. It's a beautiful thing.

I dated a man a couple of years ago who was masculine, and rich, and powerful, and attractive. On our second date, a dressy evening out, I sat in the car until he came around and opened the door. As I got out, with his assistance, he said, *"**Finally** a woman who will wait until I open the door. Most of the women I've dated have jumped out before I can get over here."*

Think about it: where and when does a man of chivalrous character, a knight, get to fully exercise his nature these days, especially man to woman? These guys honor the feminine, and want to exercise that honor if we will let them.

Ending the date: if you had a good time and would like to see him again, great. If you don't want to see him again, good to know. If you like him 51%, but there's no chemistry, consider seeing him again. Sometimes it can take up to six dates for the full complement of chemistry to kick in. If his company was enjoyable, and he treated you well, I say give it another go if he offers. After the third date you'll know if there is a shift happening toward more chemistry. If, at that point, there's still nothing, then let it go.

So let's say there is a little chemistry, and you enjoyed yourself. He'll probably ask you if you'd like to see him again, and he will either have a clear suggestion for what's next or some general ideas. You could do a little longer date next time. Still put a good five to seven days between the second and third date. Maybe next time you have a longer car time, like a 45-minute drive to a hike and lunch – let's say four to five hours together. Don't go for the full day on the coast just yet, and don't go to his home, or have him over to yours.

He may want to cook dinner for you and watch a movie at his place. Not a good idea, not just yet, for several reasons:

We want him to work to please you and make it special. He's going to cook dinner whether you're there or not, and it's much less effort than finding a nice place, making reservations, etc.

Also, going to his home, especially in the evening, is a set-up for escalating physical and sexual contact, and it's too soon.

A home-cooked dinner and a movie is a tad too long for a third date. Plus it feels a little too middle-aged and comfy. We want to keep building the juicy, anticipatory energy.

Always, you stroke and stand if he makes a suggestion that doesn't appeal to you: *"I love the idea of a home-cooked meal, and I'd like to see you again* (stroke). *But it feels like it's a bit too soon to go to your home* (stand)." You don't have to come up with another idea. Just tell him what you don't want, in language that appreciates his effort, and he'll take it from there.

Alright, the plan for the next date is underway and he walks you to your car, or gets you home, and walks you to your door. Don't invite him in. It's too soon.

If you don't want to see him again, thank him and go inside. Otherwise...

There you are. Do you want to kiss him?

That's a good thing to check in about with yourself while you are in transit to the final destination. If you do, and he invites it, go for it and easy does it. If he does not initiate it, and gives you a hug instead, okay.

However, if he's awkward, and standing there, and you'd like a kiss, and he's positioned for one, reach over and adjust his collar, then look in his eyes. That should do it.

Or you can say, *"I'd love it if you kissed me."* That should also do it.

If the opposite situation occurs, and he wants to kiss you and you don't want that, for any reason, let him know that you like kissing, but that you're just not ready for that. Most men take that well as long as they don't feel like you don't like them or you don't like kissing.

Give him a hug. Smile. Say good night. Get in your car or walk in your door, and this date is done.

Mission accomplished.

62

Why the Five to Seven Days in Between?

You need to let the oxytocin wear off, which can take a while, 72–96 hours in my experience, and then you need to think about and review the last date in a clear state of mind. How did he actually treat you? What did you find out about him? How does your body feel when you think about him? You are vetting these men, and during your breathing space is when that happens. This is also where seeing several men simultaneously packs a punch. Have a date with another guy during that five to seven-day break. It's amazing how much the ability to contrast various men helps to stall becoming overly attached to any one man too soon.

63

Inspire Don't Require: How to Enjoyably Get What You Want from a Masculine Man

Okay, so here's the deal – truth be told, you want a lot of things from him, right? You want him to take a strong lead and court you, coming up with all sorts of wonderful plans and the follow-through to back them up. You want for him to *keep* courting you once you're exclusive and more comfortable with each other. You want for him to do some things differently. You want for him to *not* do some things at all. Romantic relationships are fueled by certain energetic and behavioral dynamics. When you don't experience those dynamics, you want whatever needs to change to go ahead and change so that you will.

Then there's the small stuff, those "little" things that you think you shouldn't care about, because it means that you're shallow, or ungrateful, or a bitch, or however it is that you speak to yourself in order to discount something that's actually really bugging you. These might be things like how he cuts his hair, where he leaves his clothes or toiletries, or how he pronounces certain words, or that *thing* that happens during sex that turns you off. And it's important to be able to ask for, and receive, what you want so that you don't pull back, distance yourself, and then get critical, or codependent, or act in, or act out in some other manner. And, more importantly, this whole dance is about intimacy, which is hard to develop if you can't really say what's on your mind and in your heart.

True?

True.

So that's good. We've identified an area of intimacy that needs to happen.

However...

How it happens can be the difference between domesticating or liberating him, and decreasing or increasing his vitality and edge when it comes to making you happy. And we don't want domesticated, emasculated men, men who have learned that if they don't get it right, they get punished in some way.

Correct?

What am I talking about here?

64

How Do Women Inspire Rather than Require?

As you begin to understand how a man thinks and feels, and what matters to him in his romantic interactions, you will inevitably see that increasing your happiness is at the top of his list. And, as you expand your understanding of his personal values, you will more deeply comprehend the importance of letting him know that you perceive him to be a man of strong character and an all-around good guy.

When you keep those two ideas in the forefront of your dealings with him, they will inform your attitudes toward, and communications with, him. Here are some specific tools for implementing those attitudes and communications:

1. *When making a request of your man, come from a positive place:* "Honey, would you help me carry in the groceries from the car?" or "I'd love to see the new Woody Allen film at the Varsity next weekend. That would be fun to do with you. What do you think?"

2. **When he provides anything, make sure you stay receptive and appreciative rather than swinging into entitlement or complacency.** Even with the smallest gestures – pulling out your chair at the restaurant, giving you a nice compliment, or helping you clean the garage – give him a smile, a *"Thank you, handsome,"* or an indirect compliment letting him know how what he provides increases your well-being: *"Wow, that made my day. You're my hero," "It makes me feel so good when you tell me I'm beautiful," "Thank you, love."*

3. *Stroke and stand when responding to his lead and suggestions.*

4. *When he has blown it in some small way, let him know that you forgive him, that you're glad to see him, and that it's no big deal.*

He's late for your date, he forgot to bring home the pizza or pick up the groceries or the laundry. He's usually right on the mark with his thoughtfulness, and we all blow it now and then. If you need to, you can make a gentle request: *"Maybe you could give me a little heads-up if you know that you're going to be late. That would feel good."*

5. **Do not criticize his character:** *"You're late again? You're so thoughtless,"* or *"You forgot the groceries? That just shows how much my needs mean to you."* MMs will hear *"You're so thoughtless,"* or *"My needs don't matter to you,"* as a global indictment of their character, and they will be quick to defend themselves. *"Thoughtless? I drop your daughter off for school five days a week. I just threw a huge surprise birthday party for you. I'm taking us all to Mexico for three weeks!"*, *"Don't care about your needs? I'm paying for your health insurance, I rub your feet every night when you get home, I listen to you talk about the problems with your boss, and spend hours helping you figure out how to save your job!"*

6. **If he asks for your feedback make sure that you encourage him rather than diminish him.** MMs want you to be honest with them, and if he's asking for what you see or think, make it gentle, clear, and true. *"Well, I think that your idea to put a fence around your yard sounds great, and, given what you mentioned about the pay cut at work, maybe the timing is not quite right,"* rather than, *"You're kidding, right? You're having a hard time paying your alimony. How could you possibly afford this kind of project right now?"*

If a masculine man feels taken for granted, or expected to perform in a particular way, in other words, *required*, you can count on his withdrawal, complacency, defensiveness, and eventual loss of interest.

If he feels like you are receptive, communicative, positive, and appreciative, he will probably self-correct, and be eager to show up in a more energized and creative manner: he will be *inspired*.

Remember that these guys are generally happy, loving, generous, and deeply principled men who want to succeed at increasing your happiness, well-being, and comfort. If you keep this fact in your awareness, you will enjoy much more success at having him fulfill your needs, requests, and desires.

65

Guards Against Overinvesting Too Quickly

Once more, what we don't want is to dive too deep, too fast into exclusivity, thus allowing your perceptions to be side-swiped by oxytocin, and end up having blocked his courtship and encouraging his complacency. This is a set up for you to feel overwhelmed, unsafe, or disappointed. Your self-esteem goes down, you cease to trust yourself, and you're tired and confused.

Ick.

What we do want is vetting up front, allowing only MMs in the gate, shorter dives with plenty of time in between, and several men in the field, especially if there's anyone that you really like. Result: you feel relaxed, autonomous, clear-headed, and available for yourself and your life, as well as having some fun dates with several guys. You enjoy a nice, leisurely process of getting to know these men, while encouraging courting behaviors in them. You're energized, confident, and happy. Whoo hoo!

It's really fun to date when you're dating smart, and there's enough balance, diversity, self-worth, and breathing space in the process. These four helpful elements allow you to choose wisely, move slowly, feel mostly good, most of the time, and then be able to assess and stay in choice. Let's examine each one of them.

Helpful Element #1: Balance

Can't say enough about it: moderation, self-care, and dispersed focus allow you to keep your various priorities and interests alive and well. Friendships and family, exercise, good sleep and nutrition, fun, hobbies, passions, professional careers, creativity; whatever pieces of life experience that come together to create a whole, healthy, happy, functional you – really important to pay as much attention to them as any potential suitor (or suitors).

Helpful Element #2: Diversifying

Until you enter stage three dating – exclusivity – seeing two or more men simultaneously is big insurance against over-investing in any one man too soon. If you like someone in particular, make sure that you see other men. Keep yourself circulating so that you're in the dance as you research and discover the real potential between you. Stick to this principle. It will help keep you autonomous and centered.

Helpful Element #3: Self-worth

It has to stay high, and dating can really be a challenge to it. Interacting with men in new ways is a trial and error proposition. Men leave, or rubber band, meaning that they pull back and then reappear. Sometimes they come on strong and then fizzle. Sometimes you have a few dates, and things seem great, and then he fades out of the scene. Plus, learning new skills can be a test to self-worth. So doing what it takes to bolster your self-worth as a form of "vitamins" is important. You probably know some of the things you can do to esteem yourself: time with good friends, beautiful nature, creative pursuits, doing selfless service, strong healthy emotional connections with your close ones, reminding yourself, often, about what's so great about you.

Helpful Element #4: Breathing Space

By breathing space I mean giving ourselves plenty of time to feel, assess, and integrate our interactions with men during the dating process. Having shorter dates further apart, initially, is one form of creating breathing space. Also, taking responsibility for being as relaxed as possible and slowing down our nervous systems *while on a date* allows us to stay in touch with our experiences while we're having them. It is so easy for women to become outwardly focused and start "velcroing" to his experience. It's imperative that we feel ourselves, and have a lush platform of self-communion in order to stay honest and present with who we are, how we actually feel, and what we want and need.

Golden...

The Principles: Recap

Here is a list of basic principles that are guideposts to fun and successful early dates. They are not rules or games, but simply actions and attitudes that will bring out the best in both you and the men you are seeing. We have covered most of these ideas in previous chapters, and I have organized them into a succinct list of reminders here. You can download these principles as a series of business card-size flashcards on the last page of my website as my gift to you.

1. Look good, smell good, sound good, taste good.

2. Wear color around your face. Share your beauty with him. Wear a skirt or dress. Show some skin.

3. Don't arrive before he does: be five minutes late.

4. Let him be the guy: let him open doors, remove your coat, pull out your chair, walk you to your car, etc. Smile and thank him.

5. Ask one question to his every two. Let him fill in the silences, often.

6. Don't do his work for him. He needs chasing space.

7. Breathe, breathe, breathe. Check in with yourself. Trust yourself.

8. Stay on the optimistic side of any subject.

9. Look for the joy in everything, and share that joy with him. Let him experience your warmth and effervescence.

10. Be authentic, passionate, confident, and receptive.

11. He loves your laughter, as long as you're not teasing him.

12. Obey your sense of pleasure and comfort.

13. Relax, relax, relax.

14. Feel your body. Relax your belly. Breathe.

15. Have fun. Enjoy yourself.

16. Men fall in love when they give. Let him. Graciously appreciate and accept what he provides.

17. Remember that he thrives on contributing to your happiness. He's there to try and please you, not vice versa.

18. Get comfortable with receiving. Receiving does not signal reciprocity.

19. Give him indirect compliments and appreciate what he provides: *"I love this food," "It's so beautiful here," "Gosh, that movie made me feel so wonderful," "Your car is so comfortable,"* etc.

20. Remember that sometimes he can't think and feel at the same time.

21. Don't compete with his work. Appreciate and respect him.

22. Let him win by pleasing you. You're the jewel in the crown. He's the crown.

23. Keep your sense of humor. Smile.

24. He needs your respect, your smile, and your receptivity.

25. Slow down, sit back, relax.

26. If the conversation is stalled, breathe and wait a few moments. If he doesn't move it forward, become curious about him and find out more about who he is.

27. His work, his hobbies, his family, and his dreams are important. Ask him about them, and then listen well without interrupting.

28. If he goes on about himself, jump in, acknowledge the subject, and then relate it to yourself: *"Oh, I know what you mean about traveling. Last summer I took a trip to the Southwest that was awesome."* Remember that he gets interested in what he's talking about, and the topic should be you at least half of the time or more.

29. Don't sweat the small stuff. Be flexible.

30. If you want to, touch his arm while you're talking.

31. Trust your intuition.

32. Your integrity and sense of well-being trumps everything else. If you're uncomfortable with anything, don't do it. You never have to explain yourself unless you want to.

33. *Stroke and stand.* You have veto power. Acknowledge and appreciate his offer, and then let him know what would be more comfortable for you.

34. Keep the first dates shorter rather than longer. An hour and 15 minutes max is fine.

35. Generally, the next date should fall at least three days out from the invitation.

36. If his invitation is vague, graciously ask him what he has in mind.

37. If you want him to kiss you at the end of a date, adjust the collar of his shirt or his tie, then breathe, smile, and look into his eyes and wait.

38. Give it six dates if you like him 51%.

39. If you're somewhere you don't want to be, politely excuse yourself and leave. Always carry cab fare, lipstick, and a credit card.

40. Big self-love and self-acceptance: Remember, you're in a learning process. If you're not making mistakes, you're not in the game.

67

Third Dates and Beyond

My intention in writing this book is to help you divest yourself of the destructive effects of bonding with narcissistic caretakers, as it relates to finding and sustaining romantic happiness. In place of those past patterns of over-giving, self-diminishment, and disassociation from your own pleasure and comfort, you are learning how to reinstate the deep feminine as your personal compass, and gain a new understanding of the nature of men. We have used the process of online dating as a template for this healing and reeducation.

It is my experience that once you have gone through the process far enough to be dating multiple men and having enjoyable and successful second dates, the lion's share of the shift has occurred. Now there will be more to learn about navigating the remaining stages of dating, and moving into a healthy, sustainable, long-term romantic relationship or marriage. And there are many fine coaches and educators out there who specialize in those subjects.

When you began a journey with this book, you were probably handicapped in the area of your feminine sovereignty. Consequently, you would have been stymied by, and unsuccessful at, trying to follow the coaching of experts who assumed that your feminine energy was intact, and that you just needed to know how to apply it to their teachings. In fact, you may have had those kinds of experiences already.

But now, with all the work you have done to rewire your feminine neurology, you are on the starting line with much more health and confidence.

So in the following sections I will give you some key pieces to take with you as you move forward into the next part of your journey.

Success Watermark #2

I suggest that you take a little time to relax and acknowledge yourself for all that you just did to get a new game on, and let that game play out to the end of a second date with a masculine man.

Here are some reminders of all of the new, good, healthy stuff you've been doing:

- You made a new kind of profile with text and pictures geared toward attracting masculine men.
- You've been learning how to vet the three types of cyber suitors, discerning who seems to be masculine, and encouraging their courtship.
- You've been interacting through emails and phone calls in a manner that allows those men to court and pursue.
- You accepted an appropriate first date, and showed up and suited up in your feminine.
- You've been learning all kinds of new information that allows you to understand and interpret men in a fresh light.
- You've been willing to think and behave in ways that are new and less habitual.
- You've been getting your feminine presentation together with clothes, hair, makeup, perfume etc.
- You've been learning to keep the focus on your own comfort and pleasure.
- You've started to allow a man to make life easier for you.
- You've been letting him lead.

And, hopefully, you had a fun second date.

PART 3
More About the Men

You have learned a lot of new and useful information about men. All of that information has been in service to successfully attracting, vetting, and dating MMs. In the first two sections of this book I made the focus of the material very concise to that end.

Now that you have these key pieces in place, I'd like to expand your *man education* to include more subtle and far-reaching ideas. I believe you'll find them interesting, effective, and empowering. There is no particular sequence to these concepts. Think of this section of the book as reference material that will increase the breadth and depth of your feminine toolkit.

There will undoubtedly be some reiteration in the following pages. I have purposefully used that reiteration as a tool for solidifying important principles.

Celebrate His Lack of Domestication

Let him do what he wants to do. Just don't do anything with him that *you* don't want to do.

He needs to follow his own lead without feeling controlled or criticized. Dating a MM is like dating a bear or a tiger: their energy is strong, their instincts are usually very good, and it's really important to respect all of that.

And then there's you, and how you feel. If he's doing something that doesn't feel good to you, don't participate. It's one thing to experience preference, and another to override your core feel-good.

MMs are, and need to be, undomesticated, or possibly semi-domesticated, creatures. They have a wild streak and an intuitive brilliance that needs to flame. They have a spontaneous, bold, adventurous nature that needs to be honored continually. Letting him lead, work, and give in the beginning of courtship is one way of honoring that nature. But further into the relationship, when you are committed to one another, it is critical that you honor and encourage his wilder instincts in the form of whatever it takes for him to really get with himself. For these men, that may look like deep play of some kind: he and his buddies go off into the wilderness for an ATV holiday, he buys a hot car and messes with it, he wants to get his pilot's license, he takes serious man-cave time, dressed in sweats that you can't get near – whatever he wants and needs to do, usually without you, that lets him sharpen his edge and fuel his swagger.

Sometimes women don't understand how much these men need time away from women, time to just cut it loose and reconnect with their own instincts. This is especially true if you are in the deeper phases of intimacy, and are building a life together with more responsibility and interconnectedness. This is one area of relationship where the differences between you are keen, and you want to be on the side of his advocacy. He needs to move in and out, pull away, get relief, and organize his resources and energy around himself sometimes.

Part of a woman's job in romantic relationships is to become a keen observer of her guy's edge and joy, and to nurture and encourage whatever it is that supports those aspects of him. Obviously you hold the line morally and ethically, and you do not allow yourself to be compromised by his needs. But, short of that, let the Big Dog run, baby, and be happy about it.

70

Some Features of Undomesticated MMs

Strong, happy, playful, slightly unpredictable, high self-esteem but not vain, a little cocky in that mostly sexy way, willing to lead with potent ideas, spontaneous, romantic, likes to live large…

Needs time with the guys doing stuff that's none of our business, needs a man cave that is strictly off limits to your great ideas about how to spruce it up, a cave where he gets to keep every ugly shirt, and ripped up easy chair, and velvet painting, and beer stein collection, and every piece of technology that he wants, in multiples…

Says no when he means no, says yes when he means yes…

Takes care of his bodily needs right away, including eating, peeing, sleeping, resting, is a baby when he's sick and needs you to let him complain, moan, and be taken care of until he's well. Once he's recovered he needs for you to stop mothering him…

Does not allow you to get into his affairs, uninvited, does not like to be made fun of, does not allow you to criticize his dreams, his work, his character, or his values…

In a nutshell he does not allow you to make him your bitch…

Wants you to be happy, protected, provided for, wants you to experience maximum pleasure and fun, wants you to be his woman who is kind, confident, passionate, and receptive, will give you the world if you understand and like him…

Will study your happiness for the duration of your relationship and make it his business to increase that happiness if you understand how to receive what he's providing, digs your joy, and your self-love, and your willingness to be the jewel in the crown if you love him just as he is…

Thinks you're gorgeous and lets you know it, likes sex and wants you to have a real good time in bed, will take you when he wants to as long as you like it...

Is turned on by your beautiful smile and eyes, and the saturated colors and skirts or dresses that you wear, and the sound of your laughter as long as your laughter is not cruel, is turned on by your self-confidence...

Has a very soft heart, feels both physical and emotional pain deeply, actually more than women, will do almost anything to avoid having you be mad at him, including leaving you if he's not in too deep...

Feels defined by what he creates out in the world, in his work, his home, his toys, his family, and is proud of his achievements if they are true to his nature and his potential...

Needs a woman who enjoys yielding, when yielding is good for her, needs a woman who enjoys nurturing his body with good lunches that she packs, or folding his laundry and having it ready for him when it's time to jump into clothes and start the day, or rub his back or his head when he's tired...

He likes touch, and if she's obeying her pleasure by nurturing him, he feels loved and supported...

Kinda crazy, coyote crazy, sometimes, needs unstructured play-time, and also enjoys making a good plan and then sticking to it...

Needs for his women to dig him, and doesn't want to be anybody's fixer-upper...

Is actually available for change as long as he feels like the changes are coming from a place of increasing the good stuff between you, and it's okay if he wants to say no...

Likes to help as long as he doesn't feel taken for granted...

Needs to have his dreams, values, and character respected and valued by his woman...

Needs to have his work valued by his woman...

Likes showing off his beautiful woman in public situations, and feels like the big man when other guys think she's beautiful...

That's a masculine man.

71

How MMs Greet the Day

What follows are the motivating principles that kick into gear when generous, cherishing men roll out of bed to greet the day...

Principle #1: *"Take care of myself and my body."* Eat, pee, stretch, meditate, run or exercise, dress comfortably, make sure he has lunch covered, etc.

Principle #2: *"Take care of business."* Finish the email project he started last night, drop the car off to be serviced, handle the big meeting at work, deal with an unexpected deadline or emergency, etc.

Principle #3: *"Be a beneficial presence in my world."* Create that employee appreciation day, tell his secretary she looks nice in that new dress, help someone who needs it, increase his woman's safety, comfort, relaxation, and happiness, etc.

Principles #1 and #2 need to be in place for him to be able to devote the better part of his attention to #3, being a beneficial presence in his world, which is really the point for him. Masculine men need to feel useful, effective, and successful at making the world a better place for having walked through their day. These guys have tons of energy and vitality, and that energy and vitality will increase when they feel well-used in service to that better world. If you're in an intimate relationship with one of these men, you can count on being the primary beneficiary of lots of that good stuff.

Women can really make or break a man's spirit if that man has opened his heart to her and she does not understand and nurture his nature. Smart men will attempt to get away from spirit-breakers. But since they are very loyal to the women that they love, there will generally be some collateral damage by the time they've exhausted their capacity for giving her the benefit of the doubt.

So understanding what motivates these guys, and then learning how to help them succeed at hitting the mark based on his nature and daily motivations results in a beautiful romantic ecosystem. He will feel better and better about himself, and more and more devoted to you. You will experience the extravagant relaxation, self-love, and cherishing possible with a masculine man when he fulfills his prime directives. He will become more potent in his care for you, and you will become more deeply receptive to him, which allows both of you the possibility of falling deeply in love.

72

How MMs Experience Respect

MMs need your respect, and this kind of respect has nothing to do with power plays or dominance, and everything to do with character. He needs to know that you understand his goodness and strength of character, and that you like his lead, and that you pay attention to what matters to him, and are supportive and attentive to what makes him tick. Remember that these guys are very generous. They pay a lot of attention to making you happy because that's how they're built. They will bend over backward to increase your well-being. What they need in return is true appreciation and the kind of respect that I'm describing.

You, to him, are like a work of art that he's bringing into its fullness and beauty by applying his attention and resources. And like a sculptor with his beautiful completed piece, he is content and fulfilled by your fulfillment. And just as the sculptor would not ask his beautiful piece of art to turn around and take him out to dinner, and then go out and get a job to pay his rent, so your MM does not need or want for you to feel like you need to compromise your pleasure and well-being to make sure that he gets his.

So then, exactly what *does* he need, and how do you give it to him?

First of all, he needs for you to be warm and affectionate with him, as is appropriate for each stage of dating. Your smiles are gold, your laughter is manna as long as you're not making fun of him. He needs for you to like him as he is, and to enjoy what he provides. He needs for you to look beautiful for him, and feel beautiful with him. He needs for you to take care of yourself. When he speaks about important subjects, he needs for you to listen without interrupting. Especially important subjects will be his work, his family, and his dreams, goals, or visions. He needs for you to respond warmly when he proposes a plan, even if you don't want to do the plan.

Your warm stroke and stand:

"Honey, I so appreciate your thoughtfulness in wanting to take me to the Ice Capades. I love that you think so creatively. However, I'm not as interested in the Ice Capades as I am in something like the wine and cheese festival in Healdsberg or one of the movies at the film festival. I always enjoy trying new pairings with you, and we have great discussions after films. What do you think about doing one of those things instead?"

If he asks you what you want or need, he needs for you to tell him, clearly. He needs for you to give him the benefit of the doubt, assume that his motives are good, and don't sweat the small stuff. He needs for you to keep your word, and assume that he will, as well. He needs for you to love yourself more than you'll ever love him.

In summary: he will feel respected when you admire his character, appreciate his provision, like him as he is, listen well, respond warmly to his lead, say no when you mean no and yes when you mean yes, support his work, dreams, and goals, and ask him to step up into all he can be without criticizing him, if he asks for that kind of support.

73

Let Him Work

When women understand MMs – what motivates them, what invigorates them, what they need, what they value – dating, and eventually intimate relationships, with these guys can become joyful and fun. They do not think, feel, act, or need like women. Not that there aren't similarities. But the differences, as they play out in romance, are so significant that when we don't get it, nobody wins. When we do, a whole world opens up that is lush, relaxing, and Big Fun.

One of the primary characteristics of MMs is that they like to work for what they get. There are differences in how men and women deeply connect with themselves. In order for women to find themselves, they often have to go down and in, like Persephone. But in order for men to find themselves they frequently need to fly – fly as in use all of themselves, test their own limits, and define their actual size and nature through exertion and challenge.

I remember talking to a young male client, a vital guy in his early 20s. He talked about his desire to test and stretch his own limits in an ongoing manner within a band of brothers. His best guess was that he wanted the experience of going through military basic training. He wanted to put it all on the line in a big way.

Generally, MMs are very artfully engaged with life, and they love challenge, and adventure, and competition because they are invigorated by the kind of growth and expansion that comes through leaving it all on the field. Women are often invigorated by deep emotional connections, talking, sharing, and being supported to go deep. MMs need to understand this, and they need to learn how to support their women in this manner.

Conversely MMs need to experience all of their potential, and when it comes to courtship, they need to work to win their women.

Your escrow goes up when you allow him to chase you, to court you, and to cherish you. In the early stages of dating, it's really important that he has opportunities to extend himself toward you – space in between the dates, shorter phone calls and time together, allowing him to open doors, be the guy, pay for dates, help you on and off with your coat. He's finding, and experiencing, and connecting with valuable aspects of himself when he gives.

When women make it easy for the man to have access to her, and when she defers to his pace and preferences, he can easily lose interest, not because he's into women who play hard to get as a game, but because he needs to experience what happens for him when he's allowed to set his sights on an attractive woman and then work to win her.

74

Always Appreciate the Lead

One of the biggest complaints that I hear from smart, capable women is that within two or three months of beginning to date, the guy they're seeing stops coming up with dating ideas and plans – leading – and falls into the "what do you want to do?" style of planning dates. We don't want to be the planners – unless we do. We say we want a guy who will really take a strong lead and make great plans and implement them regularly, and we get to sit back and enjoy the ride. That's what we say.

But there are things that women do, often starting in the very beginning of the dance, which can dampen his enthusiasm for being in the lead. So let's talk about how to stay in beneficial relationship to his lead.

From the first email, one of your jobs is to appreciate the lead, even if you already know he's a guy you won't be continuing with. Sometimes it's tempting to stay in masculine "get it done" mode when you're responding to emails, which can result in you doing things like countering his date suggestions with something you like better, or accepting his idea with no real, expressed appreciation. Don't do it. Relax, breathe, and notice the lead. The email itself is a lead. He did something. So appreciate the note and any suggestions or ideas he puts out.

He says, *"Hello! I noticed your profile and just had to send a note. I liked what you had to say and you're beautiful. Take a look at my profile and let me know if I have a chance. Ciao, Ron."*

Where's the lead? He wrote. He asked you to check him out and let him know if it's a go. So let him know that you are pleased about both those things in language he understands, à la:

"Hello Ron, I appreciated your sweet note. I looked at your profile and you seem like an interesting man. I'd enjoy hearing from you."

When he calls, let him know that you're happy to hear from him. When he makes a suggestion that moves things forward, for example asking you if he can call you again, or seeing if you want to have coffee or lunch, appreciate those suggestions. *"Talking again sounds fun,"* or *"I'd enjoy having coffee or lunch. What a great suggestion."*

Every time he makes a suggestion regarding spending time together, whether it's another date idea like a movie, or dinner, or a day trip, or hike, smile and express appreciation for his ideas. This is where indirect compliments will really serve you. It's one thing to say, *"Yes, I'd like to do that,"* and that's okay. But real support for his ideas will come in the form of indirect compliments. *"Oh, I was hoping you would suggest a hike. I've been longing to get out into the open after this week at work. That will feel so good." "I love the idea of a movie. That's one of my favorite ways to relax. That sounds so fun." "Dinner sounds great. I have a new dress I've been wanting to wear. You'll be the first to see it."*

You can feel how juicy your appreciation gets when it's expressed through indirect compliments.

As time goes on, and you spend more and more time together, continuing to appreciate what he does, what he suggests, the plans that he makes, the ideas he comes up with – all of that will support his continuance of those offers and behaviors, and his provision.

Let's talk for a few minutes about what happens when you shut him down.

He says: *"Would you like to go out for a glass of wine sometime?"*
You say, **"I don't drink."**
He says: *"Would you like to take in a movie next weekend?"*
You say, **"Sorry I'm busy next weekend."**
He says: *"I saw this great New Mexican restaurant. Can I take you there on Friday?"*

And you say, **"I don't really like Mexican food."**

You can see where this is going.
And now the options.

"Would you like to go out for a glass of wine sometime?"
"What a sweet offer. I don't drink wine but coffee or mineral water would be lovely."

"Would you like to take in a movie next weekend?"
"I love that idea. I'm busy next weekend, but I have time Tuesday and Wednesday nights."

"I saw this great new Mexican restaurant. Can I take you there on Friday?"
"I love that you thought of me when you saw the restaurant. Mexican food is not my favorite, but I'd be willing to try it. I bet there's something wonderful there that I will like."

Learning to recognize, enjoy, and encourage his lead is one the gifts that just keeps giving.

75

Just Say Yes

"I'd like to meet you."
"That sounds fun."
"Would you like to spend some time on the river?"
"Yes. That would be great."
"What do you think about having lunch next Tuesday?"
"Great."

"Yes" is a stance that is open-hearted and trusting. It believes that the universe is on your side, and it enjoys the adventure of being in the flow rather than controlling.

I have a friend who married a masculine man that she met online. One of the things that I love about her is her big "yes" to life. She has a softness and an availability to what comes her way. Joyous receptivity. She had the great gift of being fathered by a man who definitely made her the jewel in the crown, and instilled within her a belief in her own preciousness and worth. So watching her very natural "yes" to life has been educational for me as a dating coach. We need our "yes," our soft, joyful "yes." It is necessary to greet the offers that come our way and welcome them with the ability to receive them. Even when we need to redirect these offers, starting with "yes" sets the scene for lots of well-being.

Practice: I invite you to try saying yes to everything that comes your way today, as long as it's not objectionable or harmful. Enjoy the adventure of letting life lead. If a day seems too long for this practice, do it for an hour. And as you practice that yes, also practice noticing what's wonderful about what is being presented.

76

How to Recognize His Protection

(Thanks to Alison Armstrong for the seminal ideas in these next seven chapters.)

As you've been learning MMs are compelled to protect, provide for, and cherish their women.

Most women can recognize the *providing* part of this equation – he will ask you out, pay for the date, and he will ask you questions and find out about your desires. He'll call you and say he enjoyed you and your time together. And the *cherishing* element dovetails with providing, and rolls over into a feeling of him regarding you as special. So let's talk about the *protecting*.

Smart women are accustomed to taking care of themselves and watching their own backs. We can handle it, or if we can't, we know who to call who will handle it for us. It can come as a shock, or, let's say, a foreign experience, when a man starts exhibiting protecting behaviors, and it's also easy to misinterpret what he's actually doing when he does it.

Here's why…

He will be thinking about you, and who you are, and what you need, and then he will be running ahead and looking to make sure that you're safe and protected in your immediate or long term future.

And here's how it plays out…

You just had a date, and it's raining, and you get to your car, and he says:

"How are your tires? Are they in good shape? The roads might be slippery on the way home."

Smart, high-performance woman thinks:
"What am I, an idiot? Of course my tires are fine. I'm a grown woman."
And she says:
"They're fine. I drive this road all the time."

She feels irritated and he feels deflated.

Smart feminine woman thinks:
"Oh, he's protecting me."
And says:
"That's so sweet. Thank you for asking. I think I'll be fine. I'll be sure to have them checked out tomorrow morning."

She feels cared for and he feels like the hero.

Which would you choose?

Learn this skill. Trust me…

77

Men and Noises

Making Noise

A lot of times men will understand and respond to noises better than words. I have a married friend who told me the following story.

"My husband and I were at an airport getting a rental car. I was waiting at the curb. When he drove up with our car I got in, and the smell of cigarette smoke was strong. I said, "John, I'm not comfortable with the smell in this car. Could you get a different car?" He replied rather ambiguously, something like, "Well, maybe we can work it out." He was loading our suitcases into the trunk. Then he got back in, and, again, I mentioned my displeasure. "John, I don't like this car. It smells bad." And again he replied, in a noncommittal manner, "Oh, well, it will probably be okay."

We just sat quietly for a few moments. Suddenly I made fists with my hands, and scrunched up my face, and loudly said, "Yuck!!!" Without saying a word my husband got out of the car, went back to the rental desk, and got us a new car."

That story made a strong impact on me. I find that masculine men seem to respond to sounds. If he is describing some wonderful plan for a date with you, try making some "*That sounds yummy*" sound instead of words to communicate your pleasure. If he's behaving in a manner that doesn't feel good to you, or proposing a plan that is not appealing, try an "*I'm not so sure about this*" sound. If you're out somewhere and you're really enjoying yourself, try making a sound that reflects this. Watch what happens.

Not Making Noise

There are times to make noise, and then there are times to be quiet. Very quiet...

When women talk with women, we have ways of communicating to each other that indicate that we're listening to, and tracking, what the other person is saying. If we're face-to-face, we will frequently do a combination of physical and verbal cues. As the other person is talking we will make eye contact, cock our head, nod, shift our bodies, and make certain facial expressions connoting, *"I hear you. I understand, etc."* Then we will often combine those physical cues with certain sounds – *"Mmmmm," "Uh huh," "Ooh,"* etc. We're actually connecting with each other through those relational cues. We like that stuff. We feel tended to, heard, and companioned when they happen.

Not so with many men. When women engage in these "active listening" behaviors as a man is talking, the man experiences being interrupted rather than being heard. He will tolerate those interruptions but he won't like them. So we need to learn to be physically still and not make any sounds while men are talking, especially if they're talking about something important. Practicing these new skills of *not doing* can really increase your man's experience of feeling respected and listened to.

If you are very quiet and still, and you just let him talk until he's finished, he will go deeper and deeper. Even if he talks for a while and then stops, even then, don't speak or move until he indicates that he's complete or that he wants you to talk. He may do several rounds of talking and then pausing. If you continue to hang tight and wait and listen, he might show you a piece of his soul. It's quite beautiful.

This is one of those situations that can cause women to, at best, be surprised, and, at worst, rebellious. It means that we need to change in order to be most effective in our communication skills with men.

Often women want men to change and be more like women. They want men to share their feelings more openly, or just listen without trying to solve the "problem," or to be able to be more empathetic and just "know what I want or need at any given time without having to tell him," etc. And we can assign meaning to what it means if he can or cannot, or does or does not fulfill those wishes. Yet those same women may not be as open to the idea that men often need a woman to change her behavior in order for a man to be at his best.

I invite you to increase your willingness to learn and adjust your own behavior for the purpose of bringing out the best in your guy, especially when it comes to listening.

78

Deeper Listening

Women often don't know how to interpret what a man is talking about when he talks about himself. When women talk about themselves, *we are often talking about what we're talking about,* e.g., *I'm telling you about my day, and I infuse the story with the feelings I experienced, and the connections that I made, and the details that were prominent to me.* We are also capable of commenting on the story as we go, moderating our experience and inner life as it applies to what we're speaking about.

So it is natural, although often incorrect, to assume that men are having the same experience when they're sharing about themselves and their lives.

Consequently, when a man goes on, and on, and on, about a subject which does not seem of interest to you, like getting the new muffler installed on his car, or cooking a seafood stew for his friend who's in the hospital, or the way his employer decided to restructure the pension plan at work, it's easy to assume that he is:

A. totally self-absorbed

B. BORING

C. so very clueless about how to talk to a woman

D. totally in his head and out of touch with himself and you

MMs very rarely do anything that is purposeless, and let's remember that their purpose as far as you are concerned is to increase your well-being, joy, comfort, and safety. They are also not vain. So sometimes they talk in code in order to let you know who they are, what they're made of, and what you can expect from them.

I was talking to a client who had received a long email from one of her cyber-suitors, and, to her, it seemed as if he just liked to talk. He chatted a lot about the recent storm, about a cooking incident where he lost power but didn't want to lose an expensive soup that was in the frig, about how various kinds of animals respond to him. She was kinda confused and disinterested.

In response we talked about this concept of deeper listening. A MM will often use a story to illustrate his character, even though he doesn't consciously know that he's doing it. I'm going to reprint the email here, with a few changes, so that you can clearly follow along with the decryption.

Hello Charlotte,

How are you today? I hope this note finds you happy and well. Thank you for your reply. I apologize for conveying all of that information about myself. Sometimes I assume that I am interesting. The power came back on last night, and was intermittent all weekend. How did you weather the storm?

The basement here flooded when the power went out, the sump pump was not able to operate. Also, the water was cut off, since this property uses well water. I had just made a large and expensive pot of egg drop soup with seafood, and the refrigerator was off. I went to the grocery store and bought ten pounds of "dry ice," broke it into chunks, and placed the pieces strategically in the refrigerator and freezer. Soup Saved!

I am curious about something in your profile, and please forgive me if I am asking the wrong question here, but why do you think that your taste in television programs is "juvenile?" I sometimes think that mine is also. Your profile leads me to believe that you are a very intelligent, diverse, and curious person. It is very appealing to me that you also have an active spiritual life.

I love most animals, but I dislike snakes. Most dogs and cats like me. I have even had a horse follow me around. I also like San Francisco, except for the parking. I suppose it is time for me to start dinner, I am going to grill a "tri-tip" for my friend that is going to have surgery

tomorrow in San Jose. By the way, I was in the Naval ROTC in
college. Take care.
Always,
Jake
P.S. Why aka "Grace"? (Grace was her cyber-handle.)

So, here we go:

"Hello Charlotte,
How are you today? I hope this note finds you happy and well. Thank
you for your reply."

Translation: She thinks he's polite, and leads with the weather, when, in fact, if we look at the character qualities behind the words, and remember his primary motivation, we see that he, initially, is kind, wishes for her best, and is appreciative of the note she previously sent to him.

He's kind, has her in mind, appreciates her.

"I apologize for conveying all of that information about myself,
sometimes I assume that I am interesting."

Translation: Now we see that he is self-reflective, aware of his potential impact on her, and transparent about his possible imperfections.

Self-reflective, aware of impact on others, able to speak freely
about his humanity.

"The power came back on last night, and was intermittent all week-
end. How did you weather the storm?"

Translation: There we see that he is aware of the natural world, and also checking in about her well-being after a massive storm.

Aware, protective.

"The basement here flooded when the power went out, the sump
pump was not able to operate. Also, the water was cut off, since this

property uses well water. I had just made a large and expensive pot of egg drop soup with seafood, and the refrigerator was off. I went to the grocery store and bought ten pounds of "dry ice", broke it into chunks, and placed the pieces strategically in the refrigerator and freezer. Soup Saved!"

Translation: This is my favorite part of the note. She thinks he just likes to chat.

Wrong.

He tells her that when he's confronted with an unexpected and challenging situation, he assesses well, notices what's of most value, and both comes up with, and implements, a creative plan that prioritizes and salvages it. And he doesn't complain, or brag, but stays optimistic and clear. He also lets her know that if he's taken the time to invest in something, he doesn't just abandon it when the going gets rough.

Deals with unexpected challenges well, keeps a cool head and handles the priorities successfully and creatively, protects his investments, stays optimistic under pressure.

"I am curious about something in your profile, and please forgive me if I am asking the wrong question here, but why do you think that your taste in television programs is "juvenile?" I sometimes think that mine is also. Your profile leads me to believe that you are a very intelligent, diverse, and curious person. It is very appealing to me that you also have an active spiritual life."

Translation: She thinks he is mildly interested in her, and, again, chatty. In fact, he lets her know that he read and thought about her profile. He's sensitive to the impact his question may have on her. He's detecting a discrepancy in the way she talks about herself and who she seems to be. He's curious about resolving that discrepancy. He gives her direct compliments. He addresses an intimate topic, her spirituality, and says that part of her is appealing to him.

Reads and studies her, likes to resolve discrepancies, gives direct compliments, cares about, and is sensitive to, his impact on others, moves toward intimacy.

"I love most animals, but I dislike snakes. Most dogs and cats like me. I have even had a horse follow me around. I also like San Francisco, except for the parking. I suppose it is time for me to start dinner, I am going to grill a "tri-tip" for my friend that is going to have surgery tomorrow in San Jose. By the way, I was in the Naval ROTC in college. Take care.

Always,

Jake

P.S. Why aka "Grace"?" (Grace was her cyber-handle.)

Translation: These are his closing statements: he lets her know that he is a good and trustworthy guy because animals like him, he likes where she lives, he attends to friends in need, and he is a stand-up guy who was service-oriented and disciplined early on in life. He gives a sweet good-bye, and handles one more discrepancy about her cyber-handle with respect.

Good and trustworthy, likes her situation, good friend, stand-up guy, service-oriented, disciplined man.

When we put all of these assets and pieces of information together, he has outlined many parts of his character and announced who he is, and will be, in relationship to her.

Good to know.

79

Dissatisfied Women Create Emasculated Men

Masculine men love making their women happy. A lot of what they do is aimed toward that end. A wise woman understands that she needs to let her guy know, in language and actions that he understands, that her well-being and joy is enhanced by his presence and provision. And it's so important to cultivate this receptivity and appreciation as a *lifelong response* to his efforts and actions. Your happiness and satisfaction is the fuel that drives the engine of his cherishing.

Just like men can stop doing the things that allow women to fall in love with them once they are exclusive, women can develop attitudes of expectations and entitlement, and stop appreciating and being pleased by a man's love. We shoot ourselves in the foot when we don't understand that an unhappy or dissatisfied woman can take the wind out from under his sails, and eventually affect his vitality, creativity, and swagger. And because masculine men are loyal beings, if you are in fairly deep, he will tolerate your attitudes and keep trying to please you, nonetheless. It's a sad thing to see.

I remember watching my Godmother, who was a wise and feminine woman, say, *"Thank you, sweetheart,"* and smile each time her husband would open a door for her or help her on with her sweater, well into their multiple decades together. It was such a sweet and vital habit, indicative of her ongoing receptivity to his provision.

Exhibiting your appreciation and happiness in response to his giving is not a game you play in order to secure his affection; it is a healthy habit of romantic interaction that brings out the best in both of you. So practice it, master it. Notice how good it feels and how much joy it produces.

80

Don't Tease Him

He won't like it. Guaranteed. *We* like it, but *they* don't.

This is a place where feminine narcissism can show up. We don't understand why they don't like something that we enjoy.

Get over it.

Often when women tease there's a little aggressiveness underneath it, and that sword can be sharp. But even when that aggressiveness is not present, teasing still carries a myriad of subtle messages. We could take all of that apart here, which might be interesting. But the material point is *just don't do it.*

MMs will tolerate your teasing in a good-natured manner for a while. But there will come a time when he will growl, or even bite, if you continue.

I once had a roommate who was a MM, a real prince of a guy. I found it funny to watch him eat. He was a high carb, throw it all together kind of guy. So his dinner might consist of mac and cheese with peanut butter on French bread and chocolate pudding. That sort of thing.

I began to tease him about his food. He took it for a couple of weeks. Then, one evening in the kitchen as I was making my comments on his cuisine, he turned to me and said, *"Stop it, Sierra!"*

That was that.

81

Don't Build Him a Clock, Just Tell Him the Time

While most women experience words as a means of deepening their connection with their man, i.e., talking about feelings, experiences, ideas, etc., men often get their sense of being connected through hanging out or doing things together, i.e., cooking, hiking, lying in bed watching TV together. Interesting, yes?

Although words certainly carry weight for men, they're often not as fluid a medium for communication as they are for women. And when it comes to needing to talk to your guy – making a request, clearing up a misunderstanding, initiating an activity or a project, expressing some feelings – brevity can be your new best friend.

If you want to talk to your man and he's involved with something else, try saying, *"Sweetheart* (or whatever is appropriate to call him), *there's something I'd like to run by you. Is now a good time?"* Remember that men are single-focused and need time to switch their focus from whatever they're doing to talking with you. If you acknowledge that he's otherwise engaged, and ask him when you can talk, he'll feel respected and give you a straight answer, like, *"No, but give me ten minutes,"* or, *"Yeah, what's up?"* He may sound a little businesslike or curt, but don't take it personally. He's just focused and interested in getting the current job done. When he's ready to talk with you, the more clear and direct you can be about what you want, what you're feeling, or what you'd like from him, the easier it will be for him to respond.

One of my clients says, *"Don't build him a clock, just tell him the time."*

Transition Time and Breathing Space

End of a long day... He's tired, you're wiped. How do you find a way to get together and let the love flow?

It's simple, but not always easy. Men and women need different things when they're depleted. If you're with a guy who works hard and is tired when he comes home, chances are he needs transition time.

So what does that mean, transition time? It means that he's switching brain hemispheres from being single-focused at work to being home with you and turning on the relational aspect of his psyche, and how he does that is *transition time*. It probably looks like some variation of barely acknowledging you, hitting the TV, or turning on the computer, putting on old comfy clothes that you've tried to throw out when he wasn't looking, sitting in HIS comfy chair, and just tuning out for a while. If he's lucky enough to have a man cave (that corner in the garage where his free weights and the 20-year old TV with the VCR live, or his office, or some sanctified portion of the bedroom where he gets to keep his stuff that you may never touch or chickify), he'll probably go there. But one way or another, he will zone out until he's back and ready to turn to you and relate. That's what he needs, and if you can leave out a post-work snack that he likes, give him a quick kiss and a hug when he arrives home, and then disappear, all will be well. He will definitely signal to you when his transition time is over by coming and finding you, by looking you in the eye and asking how your day was. He will let you know that he is now available for relationship.

Great for him, but what about you? When women are depleted they need to be pampered and filled up again. He's not available for connection, so what can you do that brings you home? This is a great time for some *breathing space* activities: a nice long walk, yoga, meditation, a hot bath. Take some unstructured time where you can reconnect with your body, let the thoughts slow down, and move into more integrated brain function. Generally, women, especially high-performance women, need some regular "me" time that asks nothing of them but to focus on their senses, stretch and relax their bodies, pet the cat, and let the mind drift. Then, when both you and he are ready, you will have a much better shot at really being present with one another, and you can enjoy some relaxed, quality time together.

83

Sex and Physical Affection

MMs need it and like it, and they need a woman who likes it as well. They thrive when they are with a woman who is generous and available with her body. This is not to say that you need to interact physically or sexually in a manner that doesn't feel good to you in order to take care of his needs. Nor am I advocating for consummated sex early in the courtship process. But I am suggesting that you understand that MMs are generally very physical guys with healthy libidos, and they'll want to share all of that with you. Down the road, when you are lovers, he'll use his sexual energy to steadily increase your pleasure and vitality. It's a huge gift that he gives.

On the first few dates, once you know that you like him somewhat, there are things you can do to warm it up: touch his arm when you're talking now and then, put your arm through his when you're walking, give him some hugs and, eventually, some kisses. Sometimes women feel like they're leading a guy on if they're physically affectionate with him before they're an item, or that her warmth may be misinterpreted as an invitation to sex. My experience is that these guys really feel connected when a woman is physically expressive, and they are respectful and grateful. Holding back physical connection is a little like holding back your smile or laughter: they won't push you to share that energy with them, but they'll probably feel a bit deflated when they're with you.

And know that as time progresses, so will your sexual contact. It's a strong part of the language that MMs speak. So if you have any unhealed issues around your sexuality that you can address without a partner, please do what you can to work on them.

Obviously this is a big and complex subject, and not the focus of this book. But I wanted to touch on it here, since it's a vital component of becoming romantically involved with a masculine man.

84

Swagger Alert

Swagger... It's the slightly cocky cousin of confidence. He knows who he is, and he feels real good about himself, and every now and again Mr. "Yeah, I'm All That" flashes his million-dollar smile in your direction. It's sexy as hell, as long as there is no cruelty or power-play mixed in. Just some big fun.

You can throw a little gasoline on the fire by letting him know that when he talks like that, or walks like that, or dances salsa, naked, while he's shaving, it's hot.

Check it out.

85

A Fun Way to Fluff Up Your Guy

These men love little notes, and short and sweet can go a long way. Get a little card and in it tell him how his presence in your life makes you feel, and cap it with a compliment that insinuates what a great guy he is, e.g., *"My life just gets better and better because you're in it. You're my hero!"* or *"Because of you I feel like a princess every day. I'm the luckiest girl in the world. I love you."* Stick the card in his lunch box, or coat pocket, or put it on his desk. He wants to know that who he is and what he does makes a difference in increasing your happiness and comfort. Let him know he's succeeded and you'll both be glad that you did.

86

Dating Older Men

It's a wonderful time to be dating if you're in your 50s, 60s and 70s. There are lots of men who are looking for partners, and lots of dating sites, meet up groups, and live singles events geared toward more mature adults. I have a number of clients in these age brackets who are in very loving, romantic, and sustainable relationships with great guys. The myth that it's over for us if we haven't partnered by the time we hit 55 is dissolving.

So what are the particular challenges that come with dating older men?

Testosterone levels drop as men age, so they can become more verbal and feeling-oriented. Our estrogen levels drop, and we can become a little more single-focused and directive. So although we are still the feminine party, to be protected, provided for, and cherished, and he is still the guy, know that sometimes you may initiate a little more, and he will share more from a heart-centered place.

Older men know what they want, what they can give, and what they won't give. Unlike younger men, who are often a work in progress, these guys are pretty set in their values, identity, and lifestyle. So listen when he tells you about himself, and believe him.

Regarding money: they want to know that you can stand on your own two feet financially, so they might list income requirements for a potential partner. It's okay. If he's a masculine man, he will still provide for you, often. He just needs to see that you're not looking for a sugar daddy.

Eventually you may be looking at a long-term future together, and that will involve a clear-headed assessment of financial viability and health care options for both of you. I would suggest that you don't eliminate an older man from your pool of cyber suitors because of his slimmer financial profile. There are many ways to creatively negotiate the future if your communication is healthy and open. But be aware that eventually this kind of negotiation may be part of the picture.

87

Securely Attached Men

This is a big subject, but I think we need to dip into it. The beautiful book, *Attached*, by Amir Levine and Rachel S. F. Heller, is a clear and concise guide to adult attachment styles as they relate to romantic relationships. Please read it. I will draw from the ideas they present and summarize the pertinent information as it informs our journey together.

We talked earlier about consistency, congruence, contingency, and companioning. Those are the elements that must be present in a parent-child relationship for a child to be securely attached with themselves, with their parents, with others, and with life. But there are also genetic propensities in the area of attachment. In other words, how we bond is molded by both nature and nurture.

Without going into a lot of the theory I will say that there are three attachment styles that are the prominent models for a person's relationship to intimacy. Those styles are anxious, secure, and avoidant. They are neither good nor bad. Genetically speaking, they were developed as a process of adaptation. I will give a quick overview here.

Those who are anxiously attached are on the high watch for whether or not their partner is still here. They are tracking energy, emotions, interactions, and reactions in the relationship. And they can easily experience anxiety or fear about their partner leaving. They want intimacy, and will bloom when well-loved.

Securely attached people enjoy intimacy, both emotional and physical, and they move toward it and work to sustain it. They are emotionally generous. They are quick to reassure their partners, and naturally expect that all will be well.

Avoidantly attached people have an aversion to intimacy. They want it. They need it. But they cannot sustain it. They are often charming and emotionally seductive in the beginning of a relationship, but soon they will begin distancing themselves from their partners with a variety of strategies.

Securely attached people often find their life partner early on, and they stay with them for life. Consequently, as one gets older, the dating pool is overly populated by anxious and avoidantly attached people. There are definitely available, securely-attached men, and frequently they will be divorced or widowed. *Attached* will help you assess your own attachment style, and gives excellent guidelines for how to vet other people before you dive deep. I urge you to become familiar with this material as soon as possible.

Soulmates in Disguise

John Gray has an excellent section in *Mars and Venus on a Date* where he talks about how soulmates often bring very different interests and elements to each other, and those different interests and elements stimulate growth and expansion in one another. Many women feel that their dream guy will share their tastes and tendencies. While enough compatibility to enjoy some shared values and activities is necessary, trying to meet men at events and activities that are centered around your interests is not necessarily the best bet for finding your deep squeeze.

I have a client who is not particularly athletic. She met a man online who was into rock climbing. They dated, became engaged, and are now happily married, and she is at the climbing gym often. Sharing this with him allowed her to get into shape and increase her overall health and vitality, majorly. His interests allowed her to forge this commitment to herself, and both parties benefited.

So here's an interesting experiment for you to try: look in the paper and choose a couple of events where there will be opportunities to mingle with and meet men, events that would not normally be on your radar. If you like poetry readings and art openings, try the edgy science expo or the Mexican cooking class at your local co-op. If friends tell you they're going to the outdoor and camping extravaganza 'cause they want to check out the new line of Jet Skis, tag along. Start putting yourself in situations where you can explore something new, slightly outside your box, and where you can meet men and ask a lot of questions. Look great, feel great, learn about a subject that you don't normally pay attention to, and see what happens.

I'm just sayin'…

Taking Care of His Heart is a Good Thing

This may sound like it's in direct contradiction to everything that I've said about *not* taking care of his feelings. Feelings and heart – two different subjects. Let's define *"his feelings"* as his emotions and how they relate to whether or not he's getting what he wants. And let's define *"his heart"* as the sensitive seat of love and tenderness within him.

When women are paying attention to taking care of a man's *feelings,* one of two things is at play... either he is narcissistic and needs for her to put his feelings first, or she is *projecting* on her guy that he is narcissistic and will punish her if she doesn't put his feelings first. If the former is true, then it's a no-win, and if the latter is true then she will compromise her feminine position with a MM. He will roll with it, but eventually he will lose his ability to continue falling in love with her. Here's an example.

Let's say that your guy wants to take you to a particular movie, but you don't want to see that movie. Taking care of his feelings would look going to the film even though it's not what you want because you think you'll get emotionally punished if you don't. And here's how the two types of men would actually respond if you stated you're preference for a different film:

NAT thinks, *"I want to go see this movie, but she prefers that one. I feel annoyed, disappointed, etc. that she doesn't want to do what I want to do."*

MM thinks, *"Oh well, I would rather have seen my movie, but she'll have more fun at the other one, so it's worth the compromise."*

Another form of allegedly taking care of his feelings might look like this:

"I can tell he really likes me and I'm not so sure how I feel about him. I should not continue to see him because I'm leading him on."

A lot of women don't want to go out with men with whom they don't feel much (or any) chemistry because they feel like they're leading the guy on.

If men started opening their hearts immediately on dates, like women sometimes do, I would say that the conclusion was a good one. But most men *don't* start opening their hearts in early stage one dating. They want to have a nice date trying to make a beautiful woman happy, and then they're done, they are able to let go and move on if she doesn't want another date. So you end up mothering a grown man and trying to protect him when he can, and will, take good care of himself. Meanwhile you don't get to be the girl and have *him take care of you*, and nobody wins.

However, his heart is a different matter. When he's experienced enough time and multi-level chemistry, and he's begun to really like you and respect you, his heart will begin to open, and that's a tender thing. MMs have big hearts, and when they open those big hearts and begin to fall in love, that's the time to pay some serious attention. It's an awareness, really, that you are dealing with a gentle giant who is surrendering a very tender part of himself to you. Maybe things will go well with the two of you, maybe it's not in the cards. But try and keep it in your consciousness that he is vulnerable at the level of his heart. I'm not suggesting that you baby him. Just consider the effect that your words or actions might have on him, and let compassion be the wallpaper.

90

The Extraordinary Power of Kindness

Kindness is big with masculine men. As I've already talked about, their hearts are tender and they thrive on feeling like they are having a beneficial impact on the world, in general, and on the woman that they care for, in particular. They risk a lot emotionally when they love. And they feel pain acutely on all levels in a way that can really mess them up if they can't get a handle on it. Even though he's not going to open that big, beautiful heart until later in the dating stages, he'll be scanning potential dates to see if he's entering safe territory. So he needs a woman who carries kindness in her eyes, her heart, and her spirit.

For women who have generally been with NATs, their propensity for kindness is often colored by either over-giving and mothering, or a brittle defensiveness. Healthy, balanced femininity is kind. It is a receptive, loving, and self-loving stance that radiates kindness from the place of fullness, joy, and compassion, the way that flowers are kind, or a summer rain is kind.

I recently started dating again. I took some prep time and had new photos done which men like a lot. A comment that I've often gotten is: *"Your eyes are kind."* That translates to: *"It feels safe to approach you."*

Whatever it takes for you to be able to connect to your kindness, please do it. It is regenerative for your soul, and a necessity if you want a healthy love life.

91

Success Watermark #3

You know a lot more about men now. You're in the process of finessing your skills and understanding of how to navigate the differences between men and women in some key areas of relationship. You've exercised commitment to releasing old perceptions and communication modalities, and you have the ability to start doing things differently.

Breathe into your own awesomeness as a woman who wants to be good to herself and the men she's with, a woman who is becoming a romantic relationship artist.

PART 4:
Girl On

So here we are…

I want to go into some more depth about you as a feminine woman, and give you more tools and perspectives that will enhance your maturity and mastery as you "get your girl on."

There will always be more to learn, since romantic relationships are an ever-evolving process. But I think these particular ideas will be potent and helpful right now.

92

From Chemistry and Compatibility to Courtship and Cherishing

When women start being courted, they find that what they want changes...

Now that you have become familiar with new models of masculine and feminine energy, and you have had some practical experience vetting and interacting with masculine men, here is a recap of one of the core principles of this work.

It's an odd conundrum. If you were raised trying to get your needs met by narcissistic parents, chances are you were never cherished – adored, wanted, valued for who you are rather than for what you do. Instead you were raised to be an adept reader of the needs, desires, and moods of others, and you learned that your worth was measured by how well you pleased those primary caretakers. The "fun" that you experienced with those caretakers probably looked something like learning to like what they liked and then doing it with them – a skewed version of compatibility.

I don't ever remember my narcissistic father saying, *"I notice that you love ballet. I'll get us tickets to see the Nutcracker this Christmas."* If we did things together, it was because it was something he liked to do and I could join him, like eating dinner together and watching TV, or taking a ride out to the desert on Sunday. And if there was ever anything that *I* actually liked, for example playing the piano, that he happened to also like, I hit the jackpot. We had some strange form of intimacy based on liking the same stuff. Girl children like me learn to equate *shared experiences with intimacy.*

Around teenage years, when hormones began to rage and sexual chemistry kicked in, that chemistry became another available form of bonding for me. An ideal guy became one with whom I shared chemistry *and* compatibility. And it was okay if I needed to work to get him to spend time and do stuff with me, i.e., court him and prove my worth so I'm the masculine party and he's the feminine, because I knew how to do that from my father's extensive mentorship.

Without intervention, that pattern just embeds itself into our identity and, then here we are, mature capable women, thinking the same way we thought as teenagers, looking for chemistry and compatibility as the magic formula for romantic fulfillment.

We often see what we expect to see, or see what we've known up to now. Women raised by self-centered parents often don't see any men except those who match the self-centered pattern. All that's possible with those guys is chemistry and compatibility, with a little strong communication skills sometimes thrown in (which will eventually get used as a weapon against you if he's not adequately pleased by you). He might start out courting you really well for the purpose of emotional seduction, but as soon as you're his, that will fade, thus leading you to believe that courtship is a set up for disappointment, and you'll default back to looking for increased compatibility.

So when women begin to do this new dance of learning about generous, cherishing men who will court them and be attracted to receptivity and women who can *be pleased,* rather than women *who seek to please,* it's common for these women to still look for chemistry and compatibility first. Of course. And if these women are willing to go out with some guys who they normally would overlook, because I suggest that they try some duty dating with courting, masculine men, it's not uncommon for these women to find out that there's a whole world of gifts that they didn't know existed. These gifts are the gifts that come with being courted and cherished. What kind of gifts? A lot of them are a kind of remembering, cellular feminine remembering... *ahh...* how it feels to be so relaxed, and feel so beautiful and confident... *ahh...* how it feels to be the jewel in the crown and have him fall all over himself, leaping across the room to open the door for me... *ahh...* how it feels to be with a man who truly gets off on my happiness and doesn't expect reciprocity... *ahh...* how it feels to have him create the secure container for me to just stay in touch with myself, and my own pleasure, and the more in touch I am, the more energized, virile, creative, and generous he becomes.

Pretty soon these kind of gifts begin to eclipse whether we're both Buddhists or vegetarians, or whether he's read the latest Deepak Chopra book. The energetic compatibility which encourages me to anchor in my feminine essence is way more fun than intellectual compatibility. Not that you can't have it all, but the whole platform shifts when you're with a man who's encouraging and supporting you to be a deeply connected and satisfied woman at your core.

93

Flexibility

This will be an exercise in loosening up. He's working to make you happy. He's into it; it drives him. You may have never had a man, or any person, for that matter, as focused on your well-being as this guy. You've been used to self-sufficiency or galpal power, and there may be some rigidity in the way you organize yourself and your life to keep things running smoothly. That rigidity is there because if life tanks there's no one but you to handle it, with possibly the help of some friends. But ultimately the buck stops with you.

So here you are in a beautiful new relationship, where you can actually relax and let someone else have your back. What that spells is a loosening up of vigilance, and with it, perfectionism.

These guys will bend over backwards to make you happy, and you need to keep that in the forefront of your mind. *Almost everything he does will be done to that end.* So your new slogan as you relieve yourself of the high watch is "How important is it?" When you can, you want to roll with the little things, e.g., you wish he would fold the towels differently, you'd prefer that he wear a different shirt, you like the other Thai restaurant better. Let him win at pleasing you. Enjoy his lead. You are experiencing the great gift of having a man adore you. Keep your eyes focused on that, and relax into noticing that he is now carrying the load that used to be on your shoulders, willingly, enthusiastically, because he wants you as comfortable and relaxed as possible. Stay there as much as you can.

There are ways to speak with him about your preferences in a manner that will honor him. We've talked about that. And, of course, if there's something that *really* needs addressing, you have to do that. But in general, try not to sweat the small stuff.

94

Become the Man You Want to Attract

Well, that's the deal, isn't it? I want some fabulous, conscious, awesome man to come along, recognize me as the GODDESS that I am, and be compelled to show me a damn good time for so long as we both shall live. Is that so much to ask?

I do believe that our romantic partners are concise and ever-evolving reflections of the way that we treat ourselves. So whatever it is that I'm wanting from HIM becomes the indicator of what *I want to give to myself.* I get to "man-up" and provide for myself the experiences, the qualities, and the stuff that I'm wanting from him.

Meaning what, exactly? Meaning that I need to see where I might be wanting for him to provide much needed playtime, or beautiful evenings on the town that demand little black dresses and four-inch heels, or a compassionate ear that allows me to talk for a long enough time that I finally get present with myself, or, or, or... And then I get to find a way to give myself those things without HIM. I get to be the inner guy to my inner gal, and take responsibility for creating a "like attracts like" condition in my vibration.

I've noticed that healthy, generous, cherishing men like to nurture and provide for women who take care of themselves and attend to their own happiness. It can get sticky when a man feels like he needs to (or wants to) rescue a woman from herself.

So I invite you to notice where you can gently begin to raise the level of your own self-provision. Maybe that means taking some risks, like traveling alone, or attending the symphony with a local meet-up group, or allotting more time in your schedule for play and then trying some new activities. Practice giving to and receiving from *yourself,* and open the space to draw in a man who is an accurate reflection of your new self-care.

95

The Grasp

Sometimes women can find themselves caught in a focused vigilance whose sole intent is making sure that *he stays*. My friend, Kira, calls this vigilance "The Grasp." Once you start liking him, and once you start receiving from him in a way that you've not received before, The Grasp can kick in.

Here's the deal: when we were little girls, ***there was one man who held the key to our happiness and well-being, and that was Daddy.*** His presence and love actually determined our ability to survive. Food, shelter, love, witnessing, protection – he was The Dude when we were four or five or six or seven. As a child we do everything we can to make him stay and give us what we need, and the wounding that occurs when he doesn't do his job very well is profound and forms the base of the original "Grasp." (By "leaving" I mean some form of substantial abandonment, which can be physical, emotional, psychic, spiritual.) His loss felt life-threatening, and often it actually *was* life-threatening. His loss put both our physical lives and the lives of our souls at risk. Our fathers should have been consistently present and nurturing for us on all levels, and they should have taught us that we were the jewels in the crown. We needed that from them.

This need is as critical to our souls as our physical survival needs are to our bodies. The fulfillment of this need allows our feminine to anchor itself in full magnetism. We have to know that we are precious, gorgeous, invaluable – we have to be taught to love ourselves more deeply than we will ever love any man, and we have to know that we are the queen. A good father would have given us all of that. When my feminine is thusly anchored, I know that I choose men, not vice versa. When my feminine is fully anchored, I allow men to approach me, to adore me, to have a shot at increasing my well-being, and I then assess whether or not they are succeeding. When my deep feminine is intact and healthy, my radiance fills me first and then spills over into the lives of those I love.

Critical.

For women groomed by self-centered parents, this set point is new land, and as we begin to arrive there, through coaching, education and new skill sets, it's a wonder. If we have not sufficiently dealt with the damage done in childhood, we can turn into grown women who encounter a deep need, this core daddy need, receiving fulfillment when we encounter MMs. When MMs start shining their provision, women start remembering and feeling their confidence and homecoming.

So, truly, this kind of nourishment and restoration to the throne awakens a need to live this way forever. And, for the moment, the guy who's reintroducing you to your sovereignty can feel like *he's* the Source of this nourishment. Here we are, rubbing up against an emotional experience that feels like Daddy should have felt, and The Grasp can engage. With it comes regressed desperation and the neediness of that little girl. Suddenly she is in charge, projecting Daddy onto another fully-grown man, and she is fearful that if she doesn't do it right, he'll leave.

Uh oh…

It's an amazing thing to be given the gift of a man who escorts us back to our station, through protecting, providing, and cherishing. The biggest gift in all of it is the realization that we *have* a station marked by deep, deep self-love, self-worth and the understanding that men are here to serve and honor our radiance, not vice versa. Not understanding and embodying this station from childhood is one of the most drastic wounds that self-centered parents enact, and the ramifications can be global.

Most of us raised by those kind of parents have spent our lives draining our precious life energy trying to earn our right to be here, proving ourselves on a daily basis in so many ways, and fortifying our self-images as women whose worth is determined by how well we give and contribute and do. It's not that we wouldn't have contributed or given if we had been escorted to the throne by our fathers, and lived from the vantage point of our satisfied grace. But we would have learned the difference between feminine and masculine contribution.

Feminine contribution is feeling-based. Our true north is our feel-good and comfort, and we give from that place. With men, often our contribution is the expression of our well-being and joy in response to their giving, and our capacity to receive, and enjoy that receiving, is critical.

Initially what MMs need most from us is tangible evidence of how well they've succeeded in enhancing our well-being with their efforts. Daddy should have instilled this experience in us, thus setting the stage for a lifetime of attracting and interacting with MMs. Instead, a narcissistic daddy teaches his girl child how to be the masculine to his feminine – how to be vigilantly attentive to *his* well-being and how to cherish, protect, and provide for *him.* We get good at it, no doubt. Here's the devastating collateral damage – when a feminine woman gives like a man, it's exhausting and depleting. We are not wired to have that outwardly-focused vigilance and giving be regenerative. We do it to get what we need in return, which is some kind of reciprocity. We give, as an MO, to get.

When we encounter MMs, for whom that masculine mode of giving *is* regenerative, we can assume that they are giving to get reciprocity, as well. Thus, we don't want to receive their giving (open the door, help you off with your coat, pay for the date) because we assume he'll be expecting to "get his" pretty soon, *as we would.* We don't know that he's actually receiving what he needs when we relax and enjoy his attention and provision because we've never encountered this model before. Or if we have encountered it, we don't recognize it because we don't know that it exists. What we have seen, and have usually attracted, are NAT men who, indeed, will be giving to get, thus rein-forcing our belief that men are selfish slime who only want one thing, and we miss the gold entirely, to everyone's detriment.

After some coaching, and practice, you will begin to exercise the new skills and principles that are contained in this book and taught by many fine coaches out there. You will choose different kinds of men, men who are good for you, and your neurology will begin to reorient itself to the receptive feminine. You will change, and your relationships will change and improve. And the possibility exists that you may still have some episodes where The Grasp kicks in. Now that you know what it is, here are some tools to deal with it:

Lots of self-care: baths, sleep, massages, time with those who love and adore you.

Feel the feelings: write about them, cry them out, hold that little girl inside and reassure her that you will never leave or abandon her.

Talk it out with someone you trust who will validate you, and who will also help ground and support you.

If you're with a securely attached MM, you can tell him what's happening. Securely attached people enjoy reassuring their partners, and they will move in the direction of communication and care.

If you find that deeper issues are being triggered, I encourage you to see a qualified therapist or counselor who can help you work through these old wounds with compassion and skill.

96

The Urge to Accelerate

This is an emotional construct that is similar to The Grasp, and it shows up like this: you like him, and for some reason a sense of urgency comes into play. There is a feeling that you need to move quickly toward more or deeper intimacy, and you may want to whip through the stages of dating, or skip some altogether. Maybe he's going to be traveling for a while, or maybe he's indicating that he would like more depth or time with you, or maybe you're just afraid that you'll lose him if you're not giving more. Whatever the reason, that urge can show up. I encourage you to be mindful should you begin to experience it. Breathe, slow down, take some time to regroup away from him.

I have found that urgency is always an indicator that I need to get with myself, pray, center, and take a little space to talk with a trusted friend and listen to inner guidance. The urge to accelerate is a yellow light. Please pay attention to it and slow down.

97

The Fantasy Bond

I'm sure there are a number of ways to approach, interpret, and define this subject, based on various schools of psychology and spirituality. This model arises from my work with Multi-Dimensional Research and Expansion, and I acknowledge the wisdom and brilliance of those gifted teachers.

Their model is this: children need to believe that they are loved, so they will take whatever behavior is exhibited toward them by their primary caretakers, be it affection, neglect, or abuse, and *call* it love. Then they actually bond with that version of love, and build neurology that desires and seeks it. When that behavior is anything other than healthy, loving parenting, the child is actually bonding with *the fantasy of love*.

The fantasy bond.

For example:
- When Dad hits me or verbally diminishes me, he is expressing love.
- When my mom neglects me, doesn't listen to my cries, doesn't feed me or change my diaper, that's love.
- When my parents belittle me for being overweight or imperfect, that's love.

You get the picture.

These children can grow into adults who actually carry within them the desire, or need for, the kind of treatment they received as a child in order to feel love.

Of course, after we've done a lot of self-examination and trans-formation, we may have weeded out the grosser examples, and healed big pieces.

However, the subtlety and insidious nature of being raised by nar-cissism can run deep. It can show up as excessive control, fear of true vulnerability, and a profound feeling of uneasiness or even anxiety when a man actually cherishes you without a demand for reciprocity. Deep, fantasy-bonded roots can have long legs, and the need to main-tain control through that identity can be such a core experience that softening it, and moving into feminine self-focus and receiving can feel like a threat.

The other most insidious manifestation of the fantasy bond springs from having had one's boundaries violated, and often decimated, as a child. Self-centered parents will use any number of strategies to strip children of those boundaries – shaming, violence, comparisons. The message is that *boundaries are bad*. Narcissistic people certainly don't want you to have healthy boundaries and limits. And likewise, *they* don't want to be defined in any way. They always want room to change, morph, alter their story, or escape.

It is the child's understanding that if they, the child, feel bad or uncomfortable, they're the problem. So these children are constantly trying to change or fix themselves in an attempt to really feel good in love. *"There must be something I can do or something I can be that will make him be nice to me, or do what he says he'll do, or hug me."*

This version of the fantasy bond says, *"If I feel uncomfortable I must be the problem,"* or *"In order to know that love is present, I must be uncom-fortable,"* or both. When a woman is subject to these fantasy bonds, it will feel like she landed on another planet when she begins dating MMs, who will both work to make *her* comfortable, and assume that if she's *not* comfortable, it's on *him* to make it right. You can see the implications. And such women may have a hard time feeling like they're being loved if that old bond isn't being played out. They often are not attracted to generous, cherishing men, and find them boring. They won't feel a spark unless they have to earn the unearnable love of a NAT.

Not good.

If you find yourself identifying with what I'm describing, and it still feels like some of this is true for you, you may need some deeper work with a qualified therapeutic expert. It is possible to heal and re-neurologize so that receiving real love and care will be the new normal, but it takes some pick and shovel work to get there. Anytime we break a fantasy bond, we come face to face with the grief, rage, despair, and disconnect that the child felt. And we have to feel our way through all of that in order to stabilize the new neurology.

It's worth it.

98

Defending the Fantasy Bond

Sometimes when women encounter these new perspectives and technologies they freak out. The fantasy bond is being threatened, and without a clear understanding of what's happening, they will regress and revert to *defending* it.

One of the biggest ways this shows up is a response to clear definitions. My work is all about seeing who you're encountering, up front, and making clear choices based on this vetting.

Women whose fantasy bonds are triggered will move over into the camp of, *"Oh, so you put men into boxes. That's a pretty narrow perspective. Everyone can change."*

That's the defense, right there.

Believing that there is something you can do to get mom or dad to change keeps the illusion of love alive inside a child-parent fantasy bond. For a child to realize that they are not loved is life-threatening, so they work with what they've got in order to survive.

If a healthy authority figure had come into your unhealthy family and said, *"This child is in a precarious situation. These are unfit parents. We are going to remove this child and place her in a healthy family."* – devastating.

Defending the bond shows up like this:

"Don't define the problem, and don't tell me there is nothing I can do to change him. You're the problem, Sierra, with these narrow confining definitions of men. How do you know what's true for every single man? Every human is different and beautifully distinct. You are not an expert on every man. There are always exceptions."

Defending the bond is a wounded child's version of love while inhabiting a 35-year old, or 43-year-old, or 59-year old woman's body.

It is defending the thinking and strategies that have reaped decades of disappointment and disempowerment.

Coming to terms with the lack of love in one's childhood is very painful, especially if the primary caretakers are still alive. And, once denial has been broken, administering appropriate consequences, when they are called for, is equally difficult. But until you do, you may continue to defend that which is blocking real love.

As I mentioned in the last chapter, for those of you who need deeper work, I recommend some sessions with a good therapist. Also, the wonderful book *Calling in the One* by Katherine Woodward Thomas is an excellent course for deeper personal excavation and preparedness for receiving healthy love and partnership.

Not everyone can do this piece of healing. But I'm guessing that if you've read this far, and are still engaged with the content of this book, you are a woman who has what it takes to do what it takes.

So do it.

Because the question on the table is:

Do want short-term relief, or do you want a stabilized shift?

99

Letting the Shadows Emerge

There is no way to encounter the new romantic goodness without having it trigger that within us which still stands in the way of receiving healthy love. If the old, displaced shadows are sitting inside of us, they are like mines waiting to be stepped on, and *kablamo*.

I like the analogy of a glass of water with a layer of silt on the bottom – when you're not involved romantically, the silt will settle and the water will look clean, and you'll think, *"I'm ready. I'm good to go."* Then, when your heart begins to engage, it stirs up the water and the silt rises, and suddenly things get murky and, gosh darn it, there are those old feelings and patterns again. If they haven't been healed, they are definitely going to surface. And even if they have been well-addressed in the past, sometimes new levels will still rise up.

They *need* to surface to heal, and if your current involvement triggers them enough, they will activate. When this occurs, the temptation is to attach those feelings to his face, and usually that's a distraction. What I mean is that you may think that you suddenly feel uncomfortable, or grief-laden, or angry *because of him*, when, in fact, he's probably the catalyst but not the cause.

I'm a big proponent of making sure that you have enough time away from your current man, enough breathing space, so that when the shadow emerges you can call it what it is, and feel it for what it is. The space will give you time to *take the face off of the feelings*. Then you'll be in a clear enough emotional position to determine if there is actually anything to work out with him or about him, or whether dealing with the feelings is strictly an inside job.

100

When in Doubt, Don't

It's your job to become more and more attuned to your own feelings, instincts, and pleasure. Like a beautiful sea anemone that opens and closes with the tidal changes, the more sensitive you become to what feels good or not, the more available you are to your own well-being, romantically.

If the initial and primary romantic dynamic is that he loves to see you lit up, and he wants to increase your happiness and pleasure as a through line, then, obviously, you have to be in touch with your own incandescence. That means you are exercising ongoing awareness of how you feel, what you like and prefer, and what effect life has on you.

As children groomed by narcissistic parents, it became an ingrained pattern to have your eyes and your senses trained outward, watching, providing for, and attending to the feelings and needs of those primary caregivers. That stance is actually quite masculine. So your parents taught you to be the guy. Because women fall in love when they receive, if you give or participate in contradiction to your good feelings, you may start to subtly distance yourself from your guy.

Coming home to your own internal compass is the journey now. More and more attention needs to be focused on you learning how to feel and gauge your own pleasure (inwardly focused), rather than on his experience (outwardly focused). If it feels good to you, whatever the "it" is, do it. If it doesn't, or if you are confused – don't. Initially, that is the practice.

101

Negotiating with Your Gut

Here's the paradox. The base camp of coming home to your feminine energy is about *feeling* good: *feeling*, as in "*my body feels relaxed and my belly feels soft and I feel secure and happy.*" And then there's the component of "*this feels right to me*" feeling good, when my ethics and intuition line up with whatever I'm agreeing to participate in (or not participate in).

As you begin to exercise new attitudes and behaviors that are at least different from, and possibly contrary to, how you've previously been operating with men, you may have some experiences which feel different or foreign. You might be tempted to interpret those experiences as being "inauthentic" or "manipulative," as opposed to "counterintuitive" because they are not yet your habitual inclinations, as if "habitual" equaled "authentic." Clearly, "inauthentic" or "manipulative" triggers a breach of ethics and intuition. And since we respond emotionally to our interpretations of life, you may respond to these new experiences, and your interpretations of them, by feeling *not* so good. You may feel tense, tight, breathless, tentative, even scared: the opposite of relaxed, soft, secure, and yummy. That's not gonna work, is it?

Even though the intent is there, and the resonance with the new material is there, the embodiment hasn't occurred yet, which leaves you somewhere in the gap on the feeling level. So, as you continue to walk through this adventure, I will encourage you to begin to study your feelings from the vantage point of knowing that you're willingly walking those skinny branches of new behaviors based on new understandings of new principles. Generally, that will mean that you'll experience some emotional vertigo, and that's a particular kind of discomfort, but not necessarily *bad* discomfort. Your job will be to begin to sort out what is appropriate, and even welcome, vertigo, and what is vertigo that indicates that you're somewhere you shouldn't be. "Progress not perfection" will be the motto, as you try new things, then self-assess and self-correct, with your increasing relaxation and pleasure being the new true north of your personal compass.

Having said that, please bear in mind that often you'll be in territory that will bring up knee-jerk responses from the old domain, responses like, *"It feels so selfish,"* or *"You're kidding me! This guy goes to all the trouble of writing me a long, complimentary note, and all he gets from me is a smile and a six-word reply in an email? It feels so rude,"* or *"I can't believe that I'm going to let this guy, who I may not really be interested in, and who makes half as much money as me, take me out to a five-star restaurant. I feel like I'm using him."* Stuff like that. You're in a paradigm shift. You're moving from your behaviors and thinking based on the old assumptions, to the behaviors and thinking based on new knowledge.

So, when those knee jerk impulses arise, please:

Breathe, notice your reactions, feel into them, and sit with them without necessarily taking action on them.

Try and reason out what you're feeling and why.

Talk to your support buddy.

Review the principles of the new model.

Ask for grace and wisdom.

Remember that, in all likelihood, what is being challenged is your sense of self-worth, and the belief that if you don't take care of his (assumed) feelings before you attend to your own pleasure and relaxation, you'll lose him or be labeled a bitch (which is an incorrect belief if you're dealing with a masculine man).

After letting yourself sit with a situation, and working with the above tools, consult your gut and trust it. If that means that you choose to respond differently than I might suggest, so be it. Ultimately you have to feel right with yourself in order to be truly authentic. I'm simply asking that you remain mindful that this journey is about shifting your understanding of how this dance works, and continuing to build the new habits and neurology that support this shift.

102

Throw Caution to the Wind

There comes a time when it's necessary to forget the principles, forget being well-behaved, and forget trying to do it right. It's a glorious feeling to realize that day has arrived.

It's not actually that you *forget* those things; it's really that you've practiced and integrated so much new information and so many new skill sets and understandings that they have become your new normal. What was once a group of ineffective habits has been replaced by a healthy perspective on men and dating. You have built effective neural pathways, through repetition and conscious choice, which have begun to kick in as new habits, habits which allow you to discern what kind of men are out there, how to recognize and interact with the healthy ones, and how to relax into being a woman worthy of cherishing in their presence.

Whoo hoo!

Once you've made the shift, you can afford to get creative. How does that creativity show up? Perhaps *you* start to approach men that you're interested in. Perhaps you take the lead sometimes in a manner that still lets him be the guy. Perhaps you follow your intuition about men in ways that create serendipity or extraordinary encounters. I wanted to drop this pebble in the pond for the purpose of supporting your own intuitive skinny branches, whenever they might show up.

103

Blessing Them All

I believe that what we put out comes back to us. Right now what you want, ultimately, is a healthy, loving, romantic relationship that feels like a blessing to you, right? Your job is to become a likely candidate for being able to receive this relationship. On the most foundational level that means that you need to *be* what you want to receive.

I like to practice the art of being a blessing force for men. I bless the guys that contact me. I bless them before they show up, I bless them as I receive their emails, I bless them as I interact with them, and I bless them if, and as, I cut them loose.

This follows on the tail of releasing indictment, and moving into a set point of kindness with men. It's the next level, and it's a preemptive attitude that positions you to be a spiritual match for that which you wish to receive.

There are two other practices of being a blessing force that I particularly love.

1. First, I like to send out a specific blessing to any man that I really like, particularly if I sense some real romantic possibilities with him. That specific prayer is that I ask for a blessing regarding his general well-being, and that he be blessed with finding the love that he really wants, whether or not that is with me. It is a psychic and emotional stance that is the exact opposite of The Grasp. I unconditionally support his freedom, his happiness, and his fulfillment, and I let go.

2. My second favorite practice is that I send out a blessing, in advance, to the man who will be my sweetheart, lover, husband, etc. I bless his life, his family and loved ones, and I just let him know that I'm here.

Both of these practices create joy, generosity of spirit, and faith within me. And they keep me centered within myself and my Higher Power. They fortify a sense in me that all is well, and that the love I desire is inevitable.

104

The Return to Sender Prayer

I preface this section by saying that I understand that you may or may not have a belief in a power greater than yourself. This prayer is especially effective for those who do have such a belief.

I am inherently spiritual, and it is best for me to keep that fact front and center, especially when I'm dealing with my basic instincts, such as companionship and love. One of the ways that I keep my Higher Power in the center of my romantic relationships is an evening practice that I call "The Return to Sender Prayer." It goes like this:

Dear God,
Thank you for this day with _____ (his name). If I'm good for him and he is good for me, please bring him back for another day. If not, please keep him, and thank you for the loan.

I think that speaks for itself.

105

If Your Husband or Partner Passed Away

If you were married, and if you loved and enjoyed your husband, you formed a covenant with a man that was deep and pervasive. Often beginning to date again can feel foreign, scary, and difficult. I've found that it's important to make sure that you break the vow with your former husband in a manner that is clear and honoring. This need also applies to women who may not have been legally married, but had a significant, committed long-term relationship with a man.

Here is a sample ritual that might help in creating a loving completion with your past beloved. You can follow it, or use it as a starting point and create your own version.

- Build an alter in your home for that man and that relationship. Put a picture of him, and perhaps one of the two of you together on the alter. Also place anything that reminds you of him, the best of him. Add flowers, candles.
- Write a letter to him, telling him how much you loved him, and still love him, and why. Thank him for all of the good that he offered to you, and all of the benefit that you received from your relationship. Pour your heart out.
- Tell him that you want to begin dating again, and that you'd like to meet another man with whom you can share a deep love. Let him know that no one will ever replace him, but you'd like to move on and open your heart again. Ask for his blessing.
- Tell him that you are formally breaking the vow of marriage (or exclusivity) that you shared, and releasing him, and yourself, to your next, highest good.

- Place the letter on the alter for a few days to a few weeks. When you are ready, read it out loud to him.
- Feel the feelings.

I think you'll find that a sense of relief and, eventually, readiness to open your heart will begin to inhabit you. You will have sown the seeds of a new beginning gently and respectfully so that you can move on with joy and gratitude.

106

Romantic Relationships as Reflections

This is a topic that is at the heart of my beliefs in regard to the purpose of romantic relationships. With many clients, our focus is on feminine energy, and moving from over-giving to magnetism. And also, as you know, I work a lot with understanding and choosing generous, cherishing men. And these are base camp skills and issues, definitely, in the dance to create lasting, healthy, long-term romantic relationships. All good.

But there is another framework for relationship that I have found to be a true vein of gold, and I would like to share it with you. This tool rubs elbows with Byron Katie's work.

There are two filters through which to use this tool; one for those of you who believe in a God, Goddess, or Higher Power of some kind, and one for those of you who don't so much. I will give you the perspectives for both. Here's how the basic tool reads:

- (More spiritual) Whatever I want from my partner, my Higher Power is wanting from me, or
- (More secular) Whatever I'm wanting from my partner, I'm wanting from myself.

So the practice is about noticing when I'm in a state of desiring something other than what I'm getting from my romantic partner, and using that as a cue to give that very thing to my Higher Power or myself, depending upon my orientation. (A note here: "My partner" is anyone with whom I am engaging in the courtship dance, from a first-time date, to someone I've been seeing, to a committed relationship, to a marriage partner.)

This is a broad topic, but it has been so valuable for me that I want to introduce it. The steps are:

Step #1: Identify what I want, *e.g., I want him to show up, be more present, acknowledge me more, pay closer attention to me, give me more of his time, energy, affection, attention, accept me as I am, etc.* Go for the roomiest definition of what it is that you desire.

Step #2: I ask my Higher Power, or my inner being, *"Is it true that what I want from him, you are wanting from me?"* Then I listen.

Step #3: If I get a "yes" I next ask, *"How would that look or what does that mean?"* Generally, I get a clear indication of what that means or how it would look.

Step #4: I ask myself, *"How can I give the very thing I am wanting to my Higher Power or myself?"* I generally do a short meditation and ask for intuitive guidance with this question.

Step #5: Once I've received the answer, I focus my attention away from trying to get something that I don't have from my partner, and I proceed to give that very thing to God or myself (or both), as I have been guided to do.

What I find is that this exercise usually results in a softening of my energy toward my partner, and an increase in my self-esteem and balance. Often, I no longer have the need to get what I thought I wanted from my partner, or he spontaneously gives it to me. I know this is a pretty juicy and possibly complex tool, but, if you're so inclined, give it a shot, and see what happens. It has changed the face of my romantic relationships, and has brought me an enormous amount of ongoing spiritual and personal growth, plus increasing tranquility and fun in my romantic life, with my guys as the catalyst.

107

A Brief Note About Personal Power

You say you want it, this state of joy, communion, and pleasure known as romantic relationship, and you have inside you the ultimate reality-producing technology. So if we put the two together, it seems that the task at hand is to marshal your internal resources and go for the gold!

At this point on the planet, science, psychology, and spiritual traditions all seem to be lining up in their agreement that consciousness is both causative and creative. If I can believe it, I can receive it...

So the question I have for you is: What are the thoughts that you habitually think about your romantic life? Are you imagining yourself enjoying the men that you are dating? Can you see yourself satisfied and joyful beyond your wildest dreams? Do you rehearse best case scenarios in your mind? Do you think of men as good, honorable, and loving? Do you think of yourself as beautiful, open-hearted, and available? How are you stewarding this precious creative resource called consciousness?

I invite you to do whatever it takes to develop your capacity for imagining the good that you wish to experience until you feel it to be an accomplished fact. Become adept at taking inventory of the contents of your mind, discarding that which you no longer want to experience, and re-seeding the fertile soil of belief with the crops you wish to harvest.

This is it. Life is no longer a dress rehearsal. It's a perfect time to accept the stewardship of this wonderful thing called consciousness and do what it takes to harness the power, presence, and creative potential inside you on behalf of your romantic fulfillment.

Let's break it down into some action steps:

Step One: Clarity. Do a little writing about what you'd like to be experiencing in this mythological relationship, and how you would feel if that experience was so. Feeling is key. Let yourself imagine the feeling-based vision, perhaps listing the qualities you'd like to be embodying when you and your beloved are together. For example, *"I want to feel relaxed, cherished, playful, sensual. I want to feel safe and open and excited about what each day together will hold."* Then imagine a simple scenario in your mind, such as being picked up for a date, or waking up in bed together, where you can assume the feeling of the wish fulfilled. Stay in the vision until you can feel those qualities, and luxuriate in those feelings for at least two or three minutes at a shot. Assuming the feeling of the wish fulfilled is the silver bullet, in terms of harnessing your co-creative power with the Universe. Practice this vision often.

Step Two: The Why. Write about why you'd like to have this experience, this relationship, and these feelings. When you focus on the "why" your consciousness has very easy access to creation.

"I want this romantic experience because it will allow me to deeply relax and enjoy life. I want it because I know my health will improve, my vitality will be strong, and I'll be living my life from a perspective of joy, enthusiasm, inspiration, and productivity. Every aspect of my life will benefit."

Step Three: Intention. Forge an intention to manifest your desire, and keep that intention front and center for yourself. Create a collage of images that inspire the feeling of the wish fulfilled. Enlist a co-creative buddy who is on the same path. Read your writing about your vision daily. Remain teachable, and avail yourself of the books, classes, and resources that will keep your vision alive.

Get this thing on its feet. It's yours if you use it, and it turns life from black and white into Technicolor.

108

Artistic Women and Romance

There is a Sanskrit word, *Shakti*, that means "power" or "empowerment." It is divine creative feminine power. When used in reference to an individual woman, it often refers to a woman's intrinsic vibrance. It is her juice, her creative energy, and it circulates through her, and enlivens and lights her up. When you are turned on, alive, joyful, inspired, and fired up in some way, that feeling is your Shakti. It is the fragrance of your femininity, metaphorically speaking, and it needs to be valued and cared for. It is your most priceless essence, and it is unique to each woman.

When we see healthy pre-adolescent girls who are beginning to be awake to life – to art, horses, the wilderness, learning, bonding with friends, whatever engages them at an essential level – we see their Shakti in a pure form. Often that Shakti gets sexualized in teenage years, when hormones kick in. It's so important to teach girls and young women how to hold and circulate their Shakti as they mature. It is meant to invigorate and inspire them, and to be shared mindfully.

One of the things that happens when women encounter generous, cherishing men is that their Shakti lights up. Spending time with a man who is self-fulfilled, happy, capable, and courting can be a powerful aphrodisiac. It's pretty darn sexy to be with such a man while he is studying your happiness and cherishing you. And it is an experience that many women have never had. The brain does its part as it cascades bonding chemicals into our systems, and it can be quite a high. Our Shakti ignites and we are radiant. Yum. I'll have another helping of that, thank you very much.

So here's the tricky part... It's wonderful to have a man in our lives who triggers all of that illumination. *But he is not the source of it.*

I need to come to the romantic arena already lit up, and that is *my* responsibility. When that is the case, his contribution will accessorize my energy, but not create nor define it. Sometimes women who have not taken responsibility for stewarding their Shakti will feel like they need a man in order to get that energetic incandescence. Never great. And it gets particularly sticky for women who are creatives.

As artists, our Shakti is designed to fill us up, and inform and inspire our creations, be they written, visual, performance, culinary, or domestic arts. Whatever our medium, our Shakti is there to grow and glow through our calling. The Shakti of artistic women is often very condensed and potent, and is designed to flow through the expansive medium of our art *first*. Then, what's left is more diluted, and can more easily be accepted and shared with a lover or romantic partner. And by art, I do not mean that you are necessarily a professional or paid artist. I mean that the creative urge is strong within you, and you follow it and fulfill it, whether anyone else ever has access to your creations or not. It is the healthy stewardship of our authentic nature that I am speaking of here.

We creatives are often very passionate people, and when we enter the field of romance, it can be a lush and rewarding experience on many levels. And if we are taking responsibility for our art, then we veer in the direction of having beautifully balanced relationships with our men. But if we are not taking that responsibility, there may be a tendency to try and run our Shakti *through* the men we're with in order to have it circulate through us, and that's not good. Healthy men can feel it when a woman is using him to ignite her Shakti, and keep it ignited, and such encounters can go bad in a number of different ways. We can become needy or dependent, and he can often feel overly responsible or, conversely, distant. Healthy men like giving, and they love to see you happy and to know that they helped. But they don't want to be used, or to feel like they're with a woman who is trying to get from him what she needs to be providing for herself.

They are sensitive barometers for these kinds of dynamics, even if they don't, or can't, verbalize those instincts.

And these guys will often treat us like we're treating our art. If we are avoiding it, he will begin exercising some avoidant behaviors toward us. If we are not giving it the time it requires, look for that reflection. If we are minimizing it, or not fully appreciating and honoring it – you get the picture.

In other words, I have found that men will reflect back to us our relationship to that which is ours to do. In this context, if I'm trying to get from him what I need to be giving to my art, e.g., time, attention, acceptance, willingness to go through the process, commitment, taking things to the next level, etc., he will often *not* give to me what I am *not* giving to my art. And conversely, when I take my attention off of him, and put it on my art, and give to my art what I wish he was giving to me, often one of two things happens – either I stop caring whether or not I get what I thought I wanted from him, or he just starts giving it to me.

We are energy systems, built to thrive according to our natures. I find it beautiful that men will assist us in that process, consciously or unconsciously. They are mirrors and romantic agents for our transformation and thriving.

109

Make Sure That You Care for the Chalice

As we looked at in the last chapter, your Shakti is the chalice – *it is the sacred vessel of your essence, your fragrance, your deep satisfied feminine.* It is that in you that energizes and awakens life, and causes vibrancy to flow through everything. It keeps you healthy and in touch with your beauty because it *is* your beauty, your radiance, your glow. Some men may try and mess with it, objectify it, or sexualize it, so it's important that you become its keeper because it is sacred. A man is only allowed into the temple if he adores the goddess in you, and to see her, and really comprehend her, he has to deeply explore and discover all of who you are. He must ardently court you, and in so doing, ardently court the Divine through you.

So, of course, *your* ardent courtship of the Divine, in whatever form that takes, is another part of the care for your Shakti, and it lays the template for his treatment of you. You must, first and foremost, organize your resources around your own Divine courtship, and then he will have the psychic construct that commands him to organize his resources around your pleasure and well-being. If these priorities are not put into place, everyone suffers.

I felt it necessary to include this idea here, because, for women who have a strong spiritual orientation to life, it's imperative that you strengthen your relationship with the Divine as you move into romantic relationship. If you start replacing your God or Goddess with a man, not good.

Only you know what it means to strengthen and fortify that relationship, according to your beliefs and practices. But, whatever it means, make sure you do it.

The higher the branches, the deeper the roots need to be.

110

The Grace Process

Whatever I do today can be infused with Grace, that invisible emanation from the Infinite which responds to my highest and best with ease...

What is Grace? I consider Grace to be the universe's ability to leap-frog over human process and move right into the full manifestation of any particular good. I personally experience Grace as an organic response to my requests and desires, if they are benevolent in nature; I ask and Grace responds. But whether or not I'm able to recognize and accept that Grace is my part of the equation.

This invisible good awaits my willingness to receive it. And in the arena of our romantic lives, things can be much, much easier, more fun, and more rewarding if we're willing to engage with Grace. So here is a five-step process for catalyzing and receiving Grace that I encourage you to try and practice. It is a practical path to using the concealed power beyond masculine or feminine energy in service to becoming *Absolutely Adored.*

Step 1: Identify the specific good that you wish to experience, i.e., *"I want to be relaxed and totally enjoy tonight's date"* or *"I want to meet a man with whom I feel feminine and happy."*

Step 2: Ask for the grace to *receive* that wish fulfilled. (A note: when you ask for the grace to receive it rather than asking for the thing itself, you are asking for that quantum force to work on your behalf, a force which is not subject to human limitations in any way.)

Step 3: Notice when the answer to that request shows up.

Step 4: Accept the good that you've asked for.

Step 5: Give thanks for the gift.

Grace is amplified when we ask for it, when we recognize it, when we accept it, and when we give thanks for it. It is powerful, transformative, and fueled by love. And it is available to you, every day, all the time.

So use it.

111

Good Endings

Paving the way for the next right relationship...

There are so many ways to end a loving encounter. What are you choosing?

Becoming conscious about the gifts received from any relationship is a blessing. Accepting and moving on with grace and gratitude is a powerful command to the Universe that you are ready for the next level of love.

I love John Gray's analogy of finding your soulmate being like the game of archery. We fire the arrows, engage with people we like, and each time we stay in a relationship long enough to have our heart open, we're given the opportunity to find out if this is the one – no open heart, no feedback. Each time we meet and fall in love, if we're maintaining healthy interactions and practicing the skills that allow intimacy to develop organically through the stages of dating, the arrow gets closer and closer to the center. Relationship is a calculated risk. But if we're not playing the game and taking those risks, we never get the goodies.

Most of my clients have new experiences of joy and fulfillment when they start applying the work that we do together. They attract a new kind of man who is generous and cherishing, and it feels good, really good. There's a thirst that begins to be satisfied which has been present for a long time. So, understandably, when a woman moves through the stages of dating with such a man, and deepens her receptivity, and opens her heart, if the relationship does not continue for some reason, it's much more painful than if the heart never opened at all. Heart open, good news, heart open, bad news. If your heart never opens, you'll never know if you've met your guy. And interacting with a number of men until that arrow finally reaches the center of the target is part of the path to finding your soulmate.

When a relationship doesn't work out, it's tempting to feel like it was a waste of time, or that you made a mistake getting involved in the first place. But the opposite is true: you're in the game, you're learning how to be the woman who's capable of finding and creating a long-lasting relationship with the right man by being willing to practice, and try, and move on when that time comes.

I want to invite you to consider celebrating the endings of relationships. Here are a few suggestions for how to create beneficial and loving romantic transitions:

1. Make a list of all of the blessings you received from your time with this person.

2. Write a letter of gratitude to that person, thanking them for those blessings, which you may or may not send.

3. Make a list of all of the opportunities that are now yours as a result of this relationship ending, and a description of the up-leveled romantic experience that you want to draw in next.

4. Create a personal ritual that releases that person from your body, mind, and spirit, with respect and prayers for your former partner's well-being.

Good endings make good beginnings. By mindfully completing a romantic connection, you inform the universe that you are a responsible steward of the love that comes to you, and you pave the way for even greater love to find you.

112

The Importance of an Open Heart

I used to be afraid of feeling the pain of things not working out romantically. In response to that fear I would guard my heart until I felt like I had some kind of guarantee that I wouldn't get hurt. That was necessary for me at that time in my life. But although it meant that I wasn't vulnerable to being wounded, it also meant that I missed a lot of glorious moments along the road.

Then two things occurred to me:

First, I can process pain pretty quickly. I know how to recognize the feelings, and let them move through me in a fairly elegant and expedient manner.

Secondly, as we talked about in the last chapter, I saw, with the help of some wonderful teachers, that if I don't open my heart, I won't be able to tell if someone is right for me or not. Ultimately, it is the heart's decision. So in order to get to the center of the circle, and meet and marry my soulmate, I was going to have to have open-hearted interactions with the men I was dating.

So then what happened?

I had to confront my fear and long-held assumptions about men and their motives. And even more deeply, I had to reeducate myself about their natures, and realize that most men are innocent, good guys. This reeducation is a primary focus of this book. I did that work, and as a result, I was able to recognize, soften, and eventually let loose the deep layers of guarding I carried inside of me. Once I was able to drop my armor and decide to err on the side of men's innocence, I found that the sooner I could open my heart with someone, the better. This doesn't mean that I don't exercise discretion, or that I over-invest or over-disclose. It's not about too much intimacy, too soon. It's really a stance that allows me to let love in and let love out, and relish each stage of this dance.

Now when I meet someone, and begin to explore with them, if things don't work out, I grieve. I feel the loss of that connection and the hoped-for possibilities. But I also feel the richness of the encounter, and the genuine care and affection that came and went between us. I use that grieving time, which isn't so very long, to honor that man and take note of the gifts given and received. Once the "ouch" passes, I assess what worked with him, and what I would look to expand or upgrade with the next man. I take some time to feel into that wish fulfilled. I bless him. I bless myself. I bless my heart, this sacred center of life and love and guidance.

And I begin again.

Bibliography

Getting to I Do	Dr. Patricia Allen
The PAX Workshops	Alison Armstrong
The Male Brain	Louann Brizendine
Mars and Venus on a Date	John Gray
Loving What Is	Byron Katie
Attached	Amir Levine and Rachel S.F. Heller
The Happiness Project	Gretchen Rubin
Parenting from the Inside Out	Daniel J. Siegel and Mary Hartzell
Calling in the One	Katherine Woodward Thomas

About the Author

Sierra Faith is a nationally recognized dating and relationship coach, author, and romantic re-educator. She makes her home in the beautiful Pacific Northwest.

Visit her at www.consciouscourtship.com.

Made in the USA
Las Vegas, NV
11 November 2021